Back by Popular Demand, with Many New Patterns and Ideas

The Collectibles Quilt II

The Complete and Expanded Guide to Creating Your Own Showcase of Memories!

by Wendy Etzel

About the Author

Wendy Etzel lives in the Endless Mountains of North Central Pennsylvania where trees tower overhead and streams cascade over rocky cliffs. Quiltmaking has served as the focus of her life for the past twenty-five years. Although her interests range from the traditional designs and colors to the more brilliant modern art quilts, she has found her niche in the challenges of portraying reality. In her first book, *Houses of Cloth*, Wendy outlines the steps that she follows when constructing her own fabric houses. Engrossing stories of the past are woven into the threads of her quilts portraying historic homes from Williamsport, PA. *The Collectibles Quilt* book inspires quilters to build fabric bookcases and cupboards which hold family photos and special collectibles. *Log by Log* encourages quilters to design primitive folk quilts focused upon the log structures of our past. Challenges of life in the early 1800's come to life through the letters of a young woman, Lydia Jane. Of course all quiltmakers need to design quilts for their beds and *The Kite Revue* prepares the stage for all those scraps and choreographs dozens of exciting designs.

In her role as a teacher, Wendy inspires quilters to design quilts that include personal possessions and depict special places. It is in this capacity that she has traveled locally as well as to Canada, Australia, and New Zealand. In 1998 Wendy was one of eight nationally recognized quilting teachers nominated by *The Professional Quilter* magazine for its Teacher of the Year Award.

Wendy Etzel
244 Lower Barbours Road
Williamsport, PA 17701
wetzel @uplink.net

CONTENTS

Jelly Cupboard - Quilt on page 48

Let's Get Personal!

The opportunity to develop a sequel to the Collectibles Quilt presented itself after a fire consumed RCW's entire inventory of books in May of 1999. Our first book, printed four years ago, had inspired thousands of stitchers to design quilts for friends and families. Meanwhile, my own notebook, filled with more exciting possibilities, had continued to expand. In addition, my stash of fabrics, filled with wood-grained cottons, now looked more like a shelf at Home Depot. It was definitely time to "build" more furniture quilts.

With a redefined mission - design quilts that have different shapes, use a variety of exciting fabrics for shelving and backgrounds, include new appliques, and above all, focus on personalizing each new quilt - I forged ahead.

Fond memories of my grandmother's summer kitchen (page 40) got me started. I scoured the house for applique ideas, uncovered a few amazing novelty prints from my stash, and headed out to photocopy some items to be transferred to fabric. After all was stitched in place, an apron was hung.

On the wedding quilt (page 42) I included half of my mother-in-law's satin dress, family wedding photos, an invitation, and lots more. The toy quilt (page 43) was the most fun. I searched through boxes of our children's books and toys, and dozens of drawings and letters that were well over twenty years old. The bulletin board on the quilt holds as many "early art pieces" as I could fit. In addition, favorite books, Lego boxes, and lots more were all reduced and transferred to fabric. Lastly, my son's favorite monkey was de-stuffed and sewn onto the last shelf. Ideas don't stop after the binding is stitched. I could have used that Mickey Mouse bed sheet for the backing and that tiny Penn State tee shirt should have been tucked into the toy basket - too late.

A hanging desk evolved as the showcase for my husband's old ties. All the tie labels were recycled as book titles and even the lamp was built from a particularly bright tie. The remains of five more ties decorate the back of this quilt (page 37).

Since December I have had breakfast with five cheerful Santas who sit upon my window sill. Inspired by a delightful Christmas card painted by Pat Richter, I was enticed to put my own Santas into a cupboard (page 48).

Although I only have memories of my doll's set of blue willow china, a magazine article lit my imagination. All the antique pieces of china were enlarged and transferred to fabric (page 41).

Judith's quilt (page 33) is a replica of her own pie safe and the tin rooster perches on her mantel; Norma's quilt (page 38) sparked an interest in genealogy and several trips to Italy; Coleen's boudoir quilt (page 45) inspired a bedroom make-over that is fit for a queen; Veronica's bookcase (page 39) was made for her husband and holds remnants of over thirty years of his life; Brenda's Southwestern cupboard (page 47) focused on family vacations in that region.

By the time this book is printed I'm sure that many more inspirations will have flashed into my head. Dig into your own boxes and photo albums to create a quilt that is bound to become a family treasure.

– Wendy

Gathering Materials

Shelf Fabric - the amount purchased is determined by the length of the wallhanging- usually *1 1/2 to 2 yds.* Wood grain prints are perfect but not imperative. Thin striped prints work well as do fabrics with very subtle textures.

Background Fabric - 1 3/4 yds for a medium sized wall hanging.The background fabric represents the dark shadow we see at the very back of our shelves. Solid black or very dark fabrics seem to fill empty spaces well. Examine the gallery section for many others.

Book Fabric - Assorted amounts - less than 1/4 yd. A wide variety of colors and textures can be used. Always keep the background fabric in mind. Very dark books will disappear when pieced with a dark background.

Specialty Fabrics - 1/4 yd. or less. Keep your eyes open for fabrics with unusual textures and pictures. Hand-dyed prints create a realistic bottle collection and large animal prints become book ends.

Decorative Trims and Ribbons - Metallic braids and satin ribbons (from 1/4" to 1" in width) are perfect for framing photographs and decorating book spines.

Threads - Decorative threads are wonderful for embroidery on book jackets. Smoke colored transparent nylon thread works well for attaching appliques.

Interfacing - non-fusible, non-woven, medium weight - This is used for making faced appliques. Fusible iron-on interfacing can be used when constructing appliques with very tiny pieces.

Tear-away Stabilizer is used whenever machine embroidery is added and when sewing frames onto photographs.

Batting - I prefer to use medium weight cotton batting as it retains its shape while machine quilting and helps to keep all those shelf lines as straight as they should be.

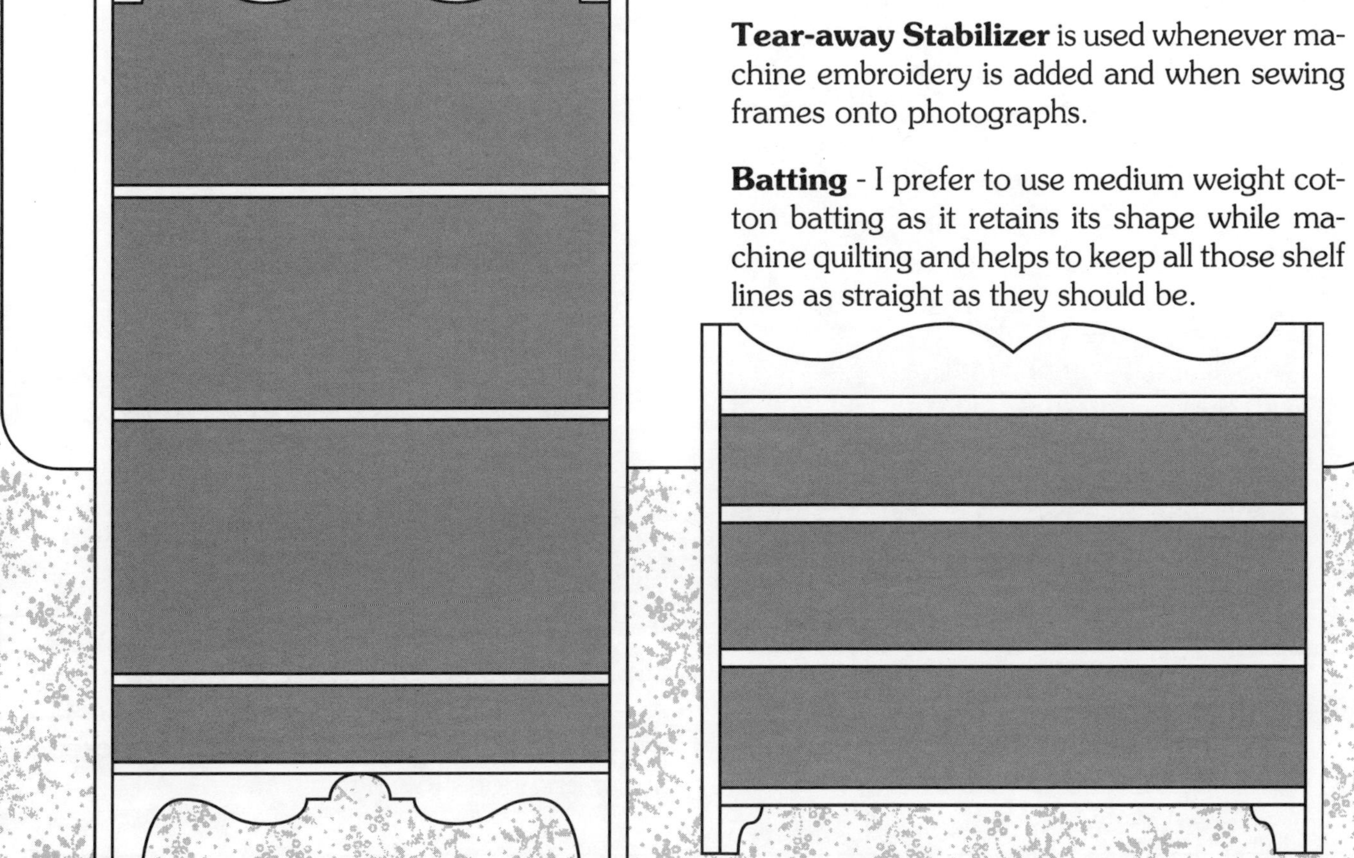

General Instructions

Making Patterns

1. Look about you and find interesting objects that would enhance your shelf. A surprising number of these collectibles can actually be traced directly onto paper.

2. Fold a piece of paper and lay the object (i.e. a candlestick, bottle, vase, etc.) so that the center lines up over the fold. Run a pencil along the side of the "bottle" tracing half its shape onto the paper below. Remove the "bottle" and smooth out some of the wiggles. With scissors, cut out the drawn shape and unfold it. Make any adjustments you feel are needed. Believe it or not, I traced teapots, bottles, toys, etc.

3. Commercial patterns for stuffed animals and dolls, as well as any of those sold especially for appliqued quilts, can be used.

Simple Faced Appliques

1. Make a full size drawing of the object to be placed on your shelf or use one of the patterns in this book (i.e. - a pig).

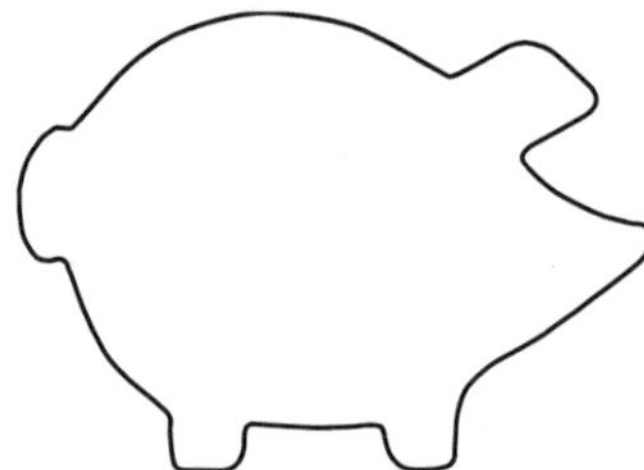

2. With pencil, trace the "pig" onto a piece of medium or light weight interfacing.

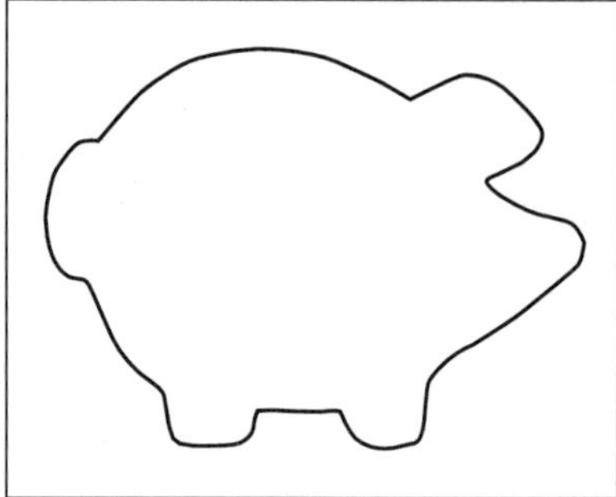

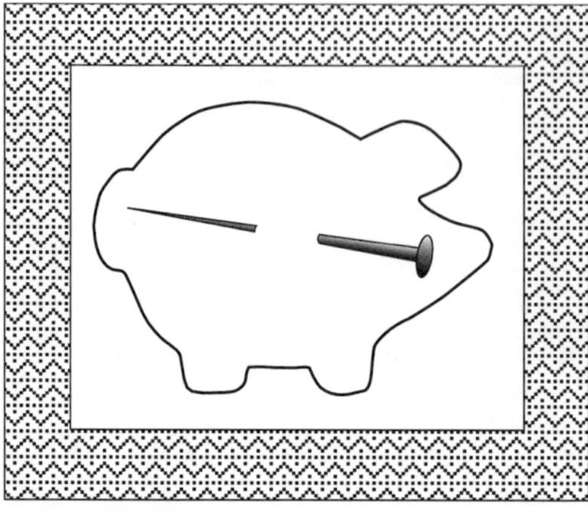

3. Place the interfacing with the drawing on top of the *right side* of the pig fabric.

4. Sew completely around the pig on top of the drawn pencil line.

5. Trim away the excess fabric along the outside edge to approximately 1/8".

6. Cut a slit in the interfacing and pull the pig fabric through the hole turning the piece inside out. Use a smooth tool to make sure all the edges are turned to the seam line. (Crochet hook, pen with retractable point, etc.)

7. Carefully iron the edges so that the interfacing is hidden under the seam.

8. Attach to the background by using hand applique techniques or machine. A narrow zigzag or pin stitch using transparent nylon thread works well. Be sure the interfacing is tucked under and not showing.

Complex Faced Appliques

1. Examine the subject to be displayed and divide it into sections that can be turned easily. (Example: the teapot will be divided into four parts: lid, spout, main body, and handle.) Follow the steps outlined on page 6 for each of the separate parts of the teapot.

2. When drawing the individual sections onto interfacing, extend those lines where the part touches the main body by about 1/2" (see ✻.) While sewing, the side of that portion that will be overlapped can be left open for turning.

3. Reassemble all these separate pieces and either hand or machine stitch them where they touch.

4. Attach your teapot to the background fabric.

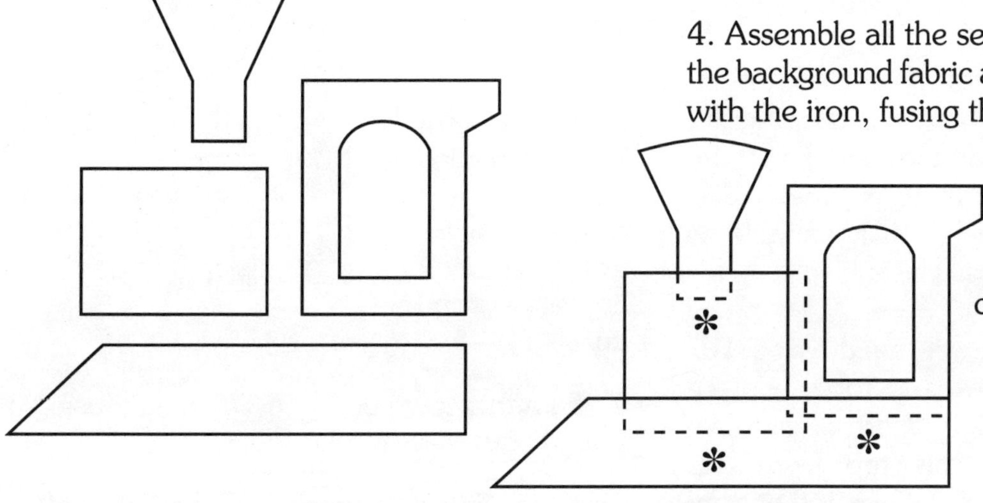

Individual sections of this engine have been faced and overlapped. The windows also represent an applique.

Fusible Appliques

Use the iron-on fusible interfacing when shapes are too small or too intricate to be handled as a faced applique (i.e. curved handles on mugs or teapots, etc.).

1. Examine your pattern and separate it into sections that will be represented with different fabrics.

2. Place the fusible interfacing on top of the penciled pattern with the paper side up. Trace the shape with a pencil and cut it out leaving a border of at least 1/4" around the penciled shape.

Note: If you want the "teapot" to face in the same direction as your original drawing, you must trace from the back side of the pattern. By turning the drawing to the back and tracing onto the interfacing against a window, there is usually no need to retrace the pattern.

3. Iron this shape to the *wrong side* of the appropriate fabric. Cut out on the pencil line and remove the paper backing.

4. Assemble all the separate pieces on top of the background fabric and carefully touch these with the iron, fusing them into the completed applique. Flip your piece to the wrong side and press it again to make sure it is securely fused.

Vertical Pieced Books

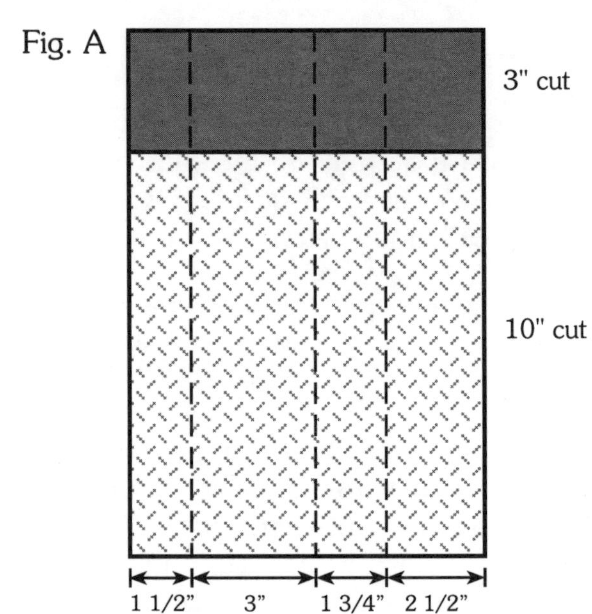

1. Construct a book unit by sewing a 3" background strip to a 10" book fabric strip (Fig. A). Press the seam toward the book fabric. The width of this unit is determined by the number of like books needed. If desired add trim or embellishments before slicing the unit. Recut this unit in a variety of widths from 1 1/2" to 3".

Note: If you do not wish to duplicate fabrics, simply sew individual 10" book slices to a strip of background fabric 3" wide. Recut after sewing.

2. Arrange a book unit for the shelf by selecting a variety of strips. Focus on choosing different colors, textures, and values. Keep the background color in mind at all times. The number of books in each unit is variable as additional books can easily be added.

3. This completed unit will need to be 10" high. Arranging these strips on top of a piece of paper that is 10" high (width is variable-12" or wider) will aid in this step. Each strip must extend to or overlap the top and bottom of the paper guide. After you are satisfied with your selection, pin these strips to the paper.

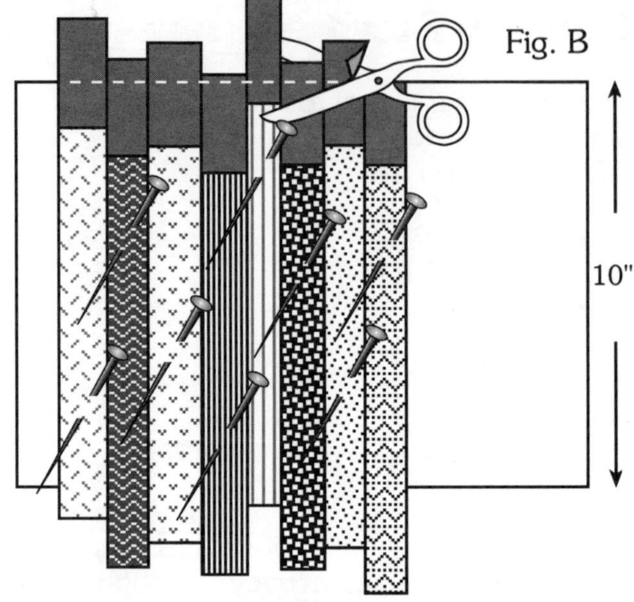

Note: Three strips of double-faced tape running across the paper eliminates pinning.

4. Trim any of the background strips that extend beyond the *top edge* of the paper (Fig.B).

5. Begin sewing the books into a shelf unit using the straight upper edge as a guide for lining up each book to be sewn.

6. Press this sewn unit alternating the vertical seams so that every other book appears to stand out (Fig. C →).

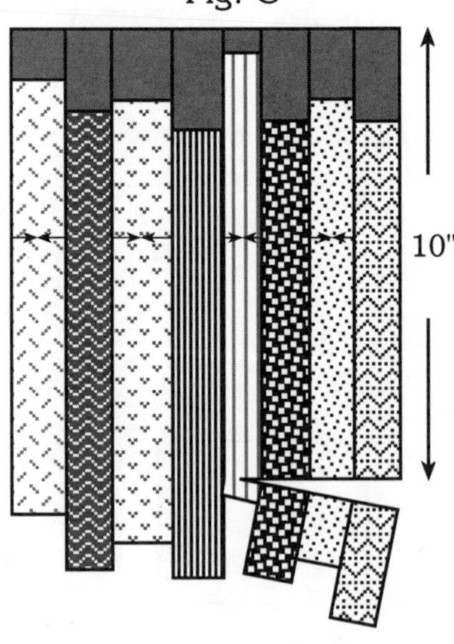

7. Trim this sewn unit to a 10" height using a plastic square or a ruler (Fig.C).

Note: This 10" height can easily be altered to fit the size you have chosen for your own shelves.

Leaning Books

Leaning books give shelves a sense of reality and serve to direct the viewer's eye to areas of interest. This placement is most effective when illustrating several volumes from a set of books. (See fishing quilt on page 36.)

1. **Faced Applique** - By constructing a number of books as individual faced appliques (see page 6), they can be placed wherever the quilter chooses. Fabric strips (books) can be faced with either interfacing or fabric chosen for the shelf background.

2. **Embellishments** - If embellishments added to the book bindings extend beyond the width of the spine, they should be stitched onto the strip before facing.

3. **A set of volumes** - Stitch all embellishments onto a rectangle large enough to yield the desired number of books. Cut vertically into individual books and face each one.

Horizontal Stacked Books

By stacking books horizontally, a stage is created for a smaller applique or photo, a book's title is more prominent, and taller fabric books can be shelved.

1. Choose books that have already been sliced from the vertical units.

2. Arrange these slices into a new unit varying their horizontal positions.

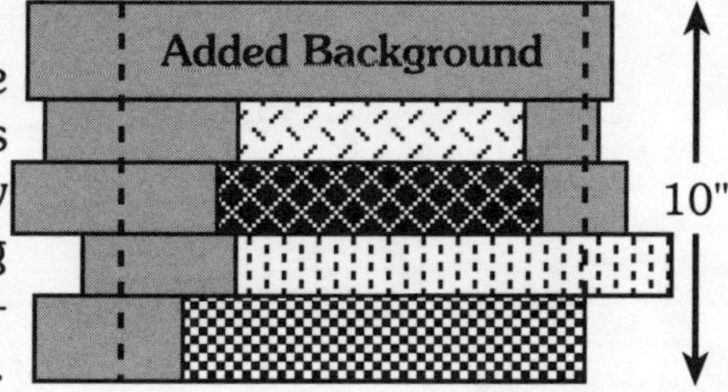

Certain positions may require a longer background piece added to the right or left of the book strip. If only a few books are stacked, a wide background strip must be added so that the unit will also be 10" high. Once complete, trim each side to form a right angle.

3. Individually faced books, as in the quilt on page 37, can also be stacked.

Open Books

1. Prepare a faced applique depicting the open pages of the book and another faced applique of a small half circle to represent the open spine.

2. Cut a strip of fabric approximately 3/4" to 1" wide and 12" long. Spray lightly with starch and iron the horizontal sides under to form a narrow strip. Working on top of the background shelf unit, position the pages and spine as in the drawing and seam the narrow strip into position tucking the raw ends under and folding the book cover slightly in the center to follow the shape.

3. This unit can be positioned with open pages on top or upside down resting on any of the other book units (see quilt on page 46).

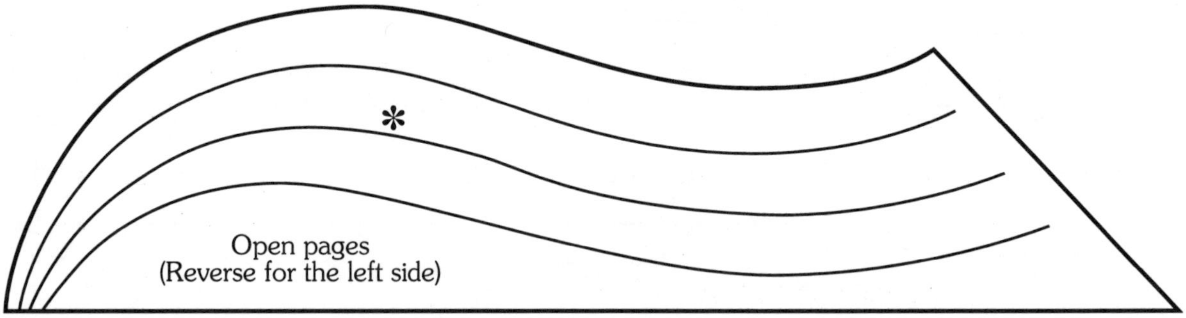

Open pages
(Reverse for the left side)

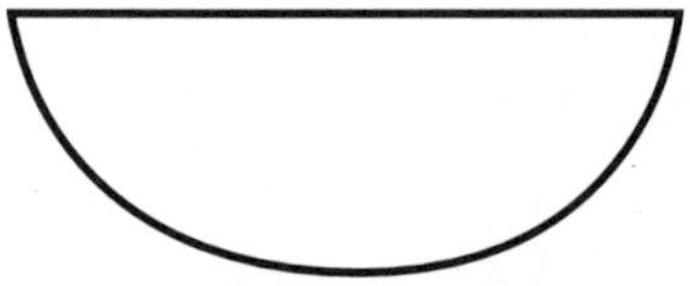

Note: Lines indicating pages can be sewn or drawn with a fine point permanent marker.

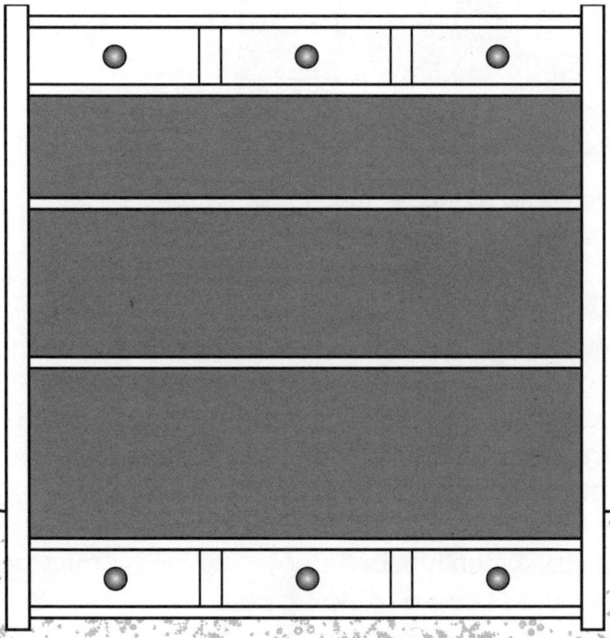

Here's a challenge!

1. **Border Stripes** - Fabrics with printed border stripes can be sliced, edges ironed under, and top stitched onto the basic book units or individual books before they are faced. Fabrics with metallic paints are wonderful for creating impressive volumes. These sets are most interesting when used as leaning books.

2. **Machine Stitches** - Decorative machine stitches can be sewn across entire book units or single sliced strips. If stitches are intricate, a piece of tear-away interfacing or other stabilizer (paper or wax paper) should be slipped underneath for added body while sewing. Experiment with machine embroidery threads.

3. **Novelty Prints** - Fabrics with printed pictures make interesting book jackets and eliminate the need to decorate. Small individual motifs from such prints (fish, birds, flowers, etc.) can be fused to the spines of books.

4. **Photo Transfers** - Photocopy a colorful book jacket and transfer it to fabric. This "book" could be placed on the shelf with the front cover in full view. On the toy quilt (page 43), I have included the covers of favorite worn books from my children's past as well as opened pages where text is visible.

5. **Children's Cloth Books** - Perhaps you still have a child's cloth book. The cover or specific pages could be treated as an applique and added to a child's quilt.

6. **Fabrics with a history** - Men's ties (page 37), old aprons, children's clothing, or pieces of a prom dress can be transformed into books and appliques. Ribbons awarded as prizes (county fairs, quilt contests, dog shows, etc.) are easily faced and placed on a shelf.

7. **Book Titles** - Favorite book titles can be embroidered by hand or machine. With the help of her brother and the "kids", Lynn Parker of Los Alamos, New Mexico, assigned very special titles to each of her books. Enjoy!

- **Power to the People** – *my brother is CEO of a power cooperative*
- **I Give a Hoot and a Holler** – *my niece counts owls in the Oregon forest*
- **This New House** – *my brother and sister-in-law have spent 4 years remodeling their house*
- **Psychotics Are People Too** – *my niece is working on a doctor's degree in psychology*
- **The Hammer and the Thumb** – *my nephew is in construction engineering in college*
- **Jurisprudence and You** – *my niece just got her jurisprudence degree*
- **Search for the Perfect Scrap** – *my grandma and me, quilters*
- **The Psychology of Smart Investing** – *my husband does a lot with commodities*
- **Fields and Streams** – *my son is with a firm that restores wetlands*
- **Oklahoma with Style** – *my daughter is a graphic designer in Oklahoma City*
- **Hard Bodies in 5 Hours a Day** – *my niece does something with nutrition and exercise*
- **My Life in Wood Grains** – *my dad (now deceased) did a lot of woodwork and furniture building*
- For my mother –
  - **Golf, the Spectator Sport** – *she enjoys watching it on TV*
  - **Better Homes and Gardens Cookbook** – *the one with the red plaid cover*
  - **To Dance with a White Dog** – *Mom's favorite novel*
  - **The Bible**
  - **Concordance**
  - **The New Testament**
  - **Birds**
  - **1001 Very Difficult Crosswords**
  - **Point Count Bidding**

Photographs

1. Sort through all those old photographs in the attic and choose those that you intend to use. Examine the sizes of your prints. 8 x 10's will probably need to be reduced slightly to 6" x 8" and others may be enlarged. It is easiest to work with a variety of sizes so that you can group photos and place smaller pictures in front of larger ones, as you would on an actual shelf.

2. Have your photos transferred to fabric. There are several companies that specialize in this procedure. Special papers can be purchased and used in conjunction with a color copier or home computer. After the images are printed onto paper, they can be transferred to cloth at home with an iron. I used *Photo Effects* distributed by TransferMagic.com (1-800-268-9841). In addition, there are companies that will transfer your photos for you. Check photo stores and listings in quilt magazines.

3. Group and arrange your fabric photos on top of the background fabric you have decided on using. In order to present an interesting arrangement with some perspective, several of the photos might overlap each other. By examining magazines and especially catalogs in which frames are advertized, you will find some guidance. Examine some of these examples in figures A and B.

Fig. A

Fig. B

4. Trim the excess muslin from around the fabric photo so that only 1/4" remains.

5. Place the photo on a larger piece of tear-away stabilizer. Any sewing on this frame must be done on top of this base as the ribbons and metallic trims will cause the photo to pucker without it.

6. If you are going to slant this particular picture, draw the angle using a pencil and ruler. I have chosen to slant only the top and bottom edges, allowing the sides to remain perpendicular to the shelf. Trim the photograph allowing 1/4" to remain beyond the drawn lines.

7. Choose from your satin ribbons and trims to select a picture frame. Gold and silver trims are great but must be flexible enough to be folded when turning the corners.

8. Begin on a corner that will eventually be overlapped by another photo or a corner that will touch the lower shelf board where the raw edge can be caught in the seam. (See *)

9. Carefully top stitch the ribbon to the fabric photo along the inner edge. As you come to a corner, fold the ribbon or trim with a pin or seam ripper so that a mitered corner is formed.

10. Ribbons can be layered and metallic trims can be stitched along the outer edges of the ribbon.

11. Once complete, remove the stabilizer carefully. Turn the photo over and make a small slit in the stabilizer. Slip the rounded point of the seam ripper into the slit and carefully follow the stitching. I allow the stabilizer to remain between the very narrow parallel seams.

12. Lastly, the framed photos can be placed on the background fabric and top stitched by machine. Usually I use a straight stitch and sew very close to the outer edge. When sewing over metallic trims a slight zig-zag with thread to match the background works well.

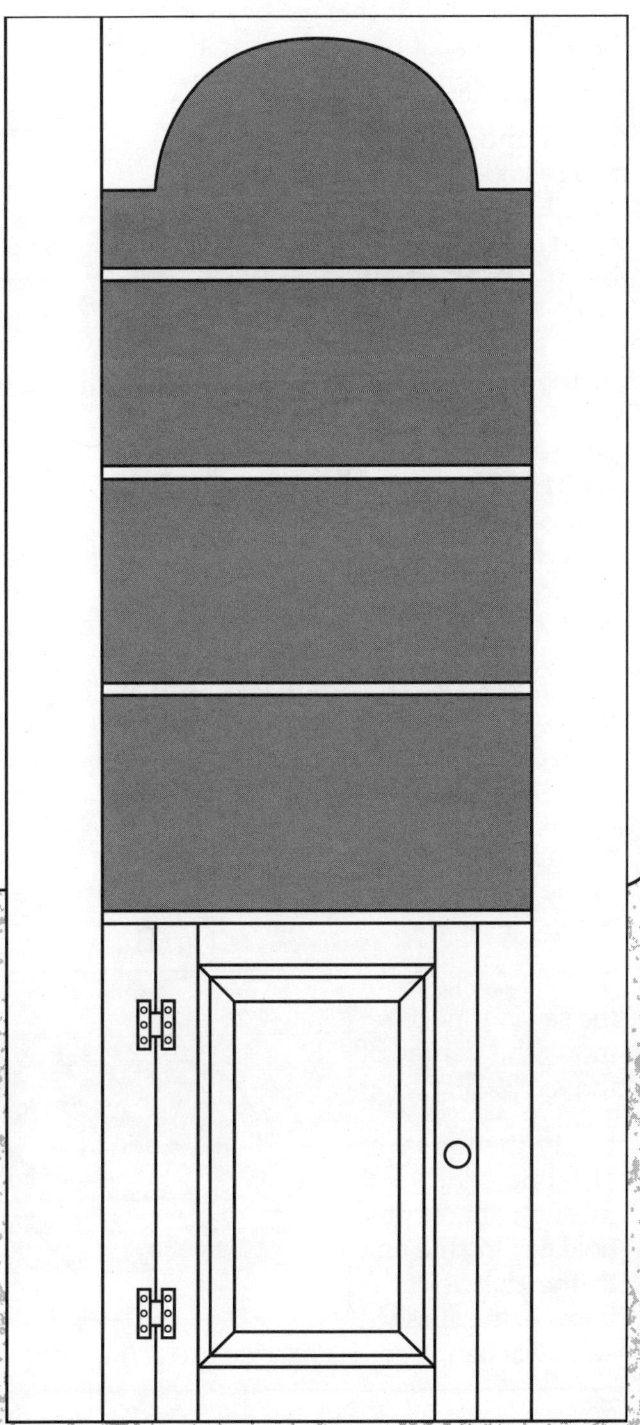

Plates, Mirrors and Oval Picture Frames

In order to replicate a realistic plate or mirror, it is necessary to use two fabrics, one for the center and another to represent the outer band or frame. An example can be seen on the top shelf of the Family quilt (plate) on page 44 and the Wedding quilt (mirror) on page 42. (Note: A shiny metallic knit was used for the mirror.)

1. Choose a printed fabric with a design that reminds you of a decorated plate and a plainer background fabric that will be used for the outer band. These inner and outer fabric positions can be switched.

Fig.A

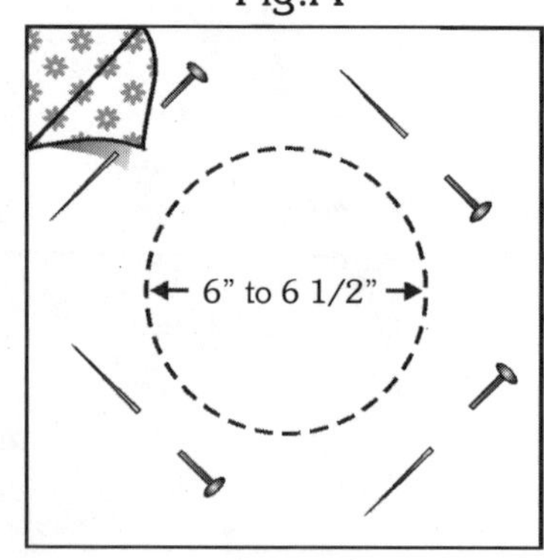

2. In making a **plate** you first will be making a faced circular frame to be used as the outer band. Cut two 11" squares of the fabric chosen for the outer band. With their *right sides together*, trace the circumference of a circle 6" to 6 1/2" onto the top square. Search your cupboards for a dish, lid, pie pan, etc. to be used as a template. (Fig. A) **Mirror**: If you are making a mirror frame the two pieces of frame fabric must be at least 3" larger than your paper drawing. Layer the two fabrics and pin the paper drawing to the fabrics.

3. Pin the two layers together and machine stitch on top of the drawn circle or inner edge of the frame. Carefully remove the paper mirror retaining its shape.

Fig. B

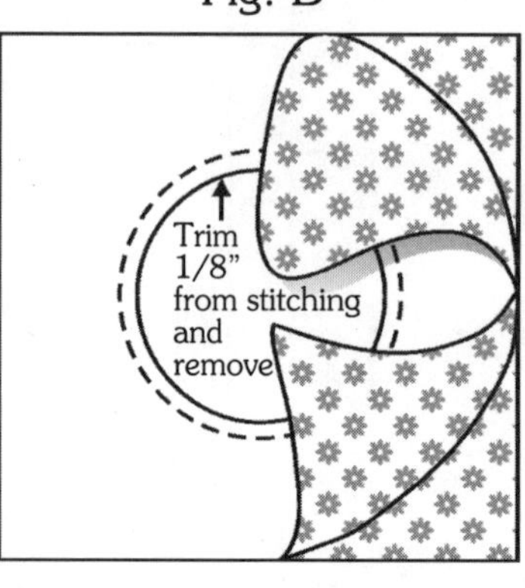

4. Cut 1/8" from the sewing line to remove the center of the circle. (Fig. B)

5. Lift the top layer of fabric and pull it through the center hole turning the unit to the right side. A frame with a finished edge will be formed. Press carefully. (Fig. B)

Fig C

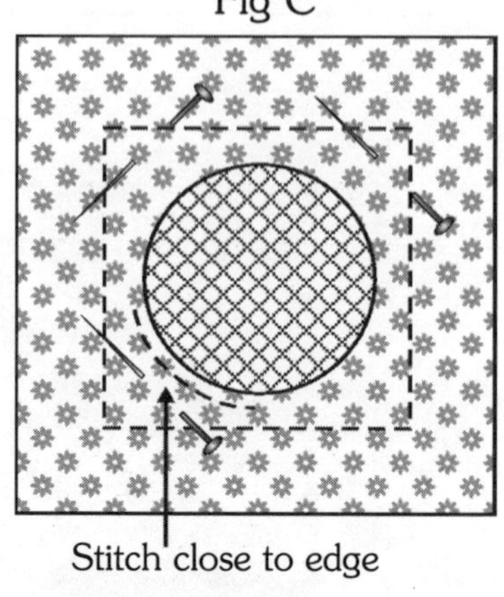

6. Place this circular frame over the fabric you have chosen for the center of the plate or mirror; pin and top stitch along the turned edge of this inner circle. Trim away the excess fabric from behind. (Fig. C)

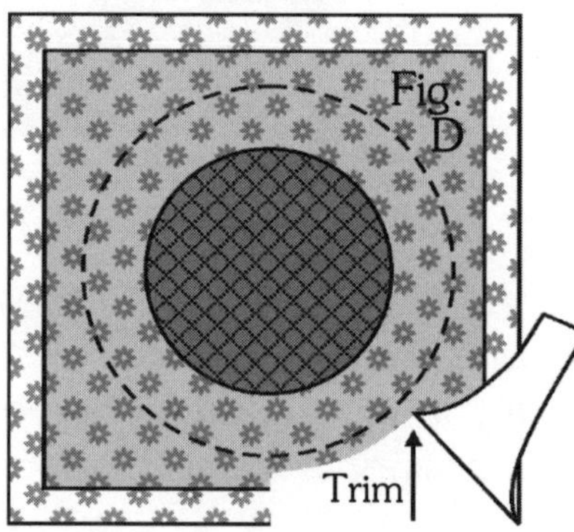

7. With a pencil trace a larger circle (8" to 8-1/2") onto interfacing (medium weight, non-woven, nonfusible). Pin the interfacing on top of the plate (right side up), centering the larger circle over the smaller inner circle. (Fig. D) **Mirror**: Trace the outer edge of the mirror onto interfacing and follow the instructions above.

8. Stitch on top of the pencil line. Trim the outer edge approximately 1/8" from the sewn line. (Fig. D)

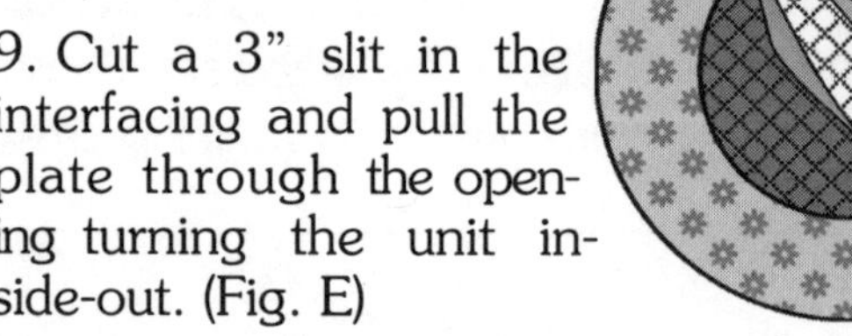

9. Cut a 3" slit in the interfacing and pull the plate through the opening turning the unit inside-out. (Fig. E)

10. Iron carefully, making sure the outer circle is smooth.

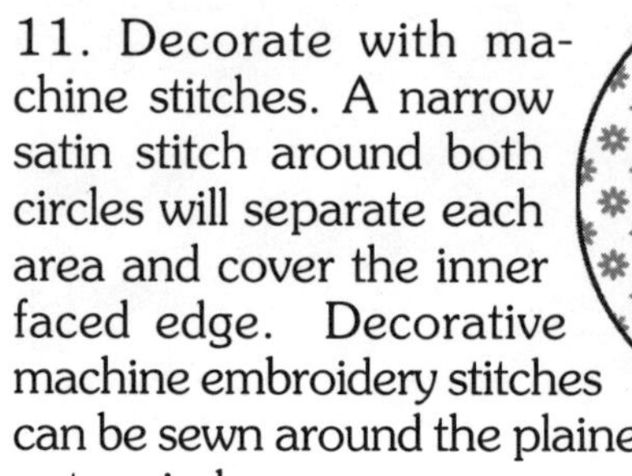

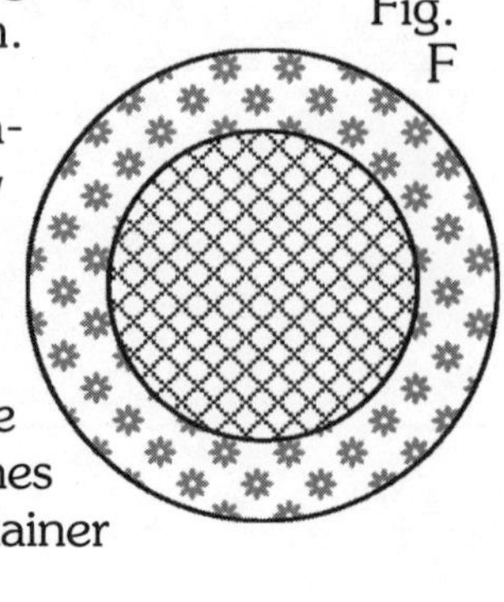

11. Decorate with machine stitches. A narrow satin stitch around both circles will separate each area and cover the inner faced edge. Decorative machine embroidery stitches can be sewn around the plainer outer circle.

Pie Safe Quilts

1. Trace the pierced design onto interfacing (non-woven, non-fusible).

2. Layer the "tin" fabric (right side out), thin batting, and interfacing (design side down), as you would a quilt. Pin.

3. Turn to the reverse side and machine stitch over the traced design on the interfacing using black thread. Experiment with decorative stitches to best represent the punched design. The pattern will be reproduced on the right side with the bobbin thread. (See page 16.)

Note: Hand stitching with embroidery thread would also work well.

4. Size and trim the panels and begin the construction of the pie safe doors. Refer to the drawing or design your very own antique.

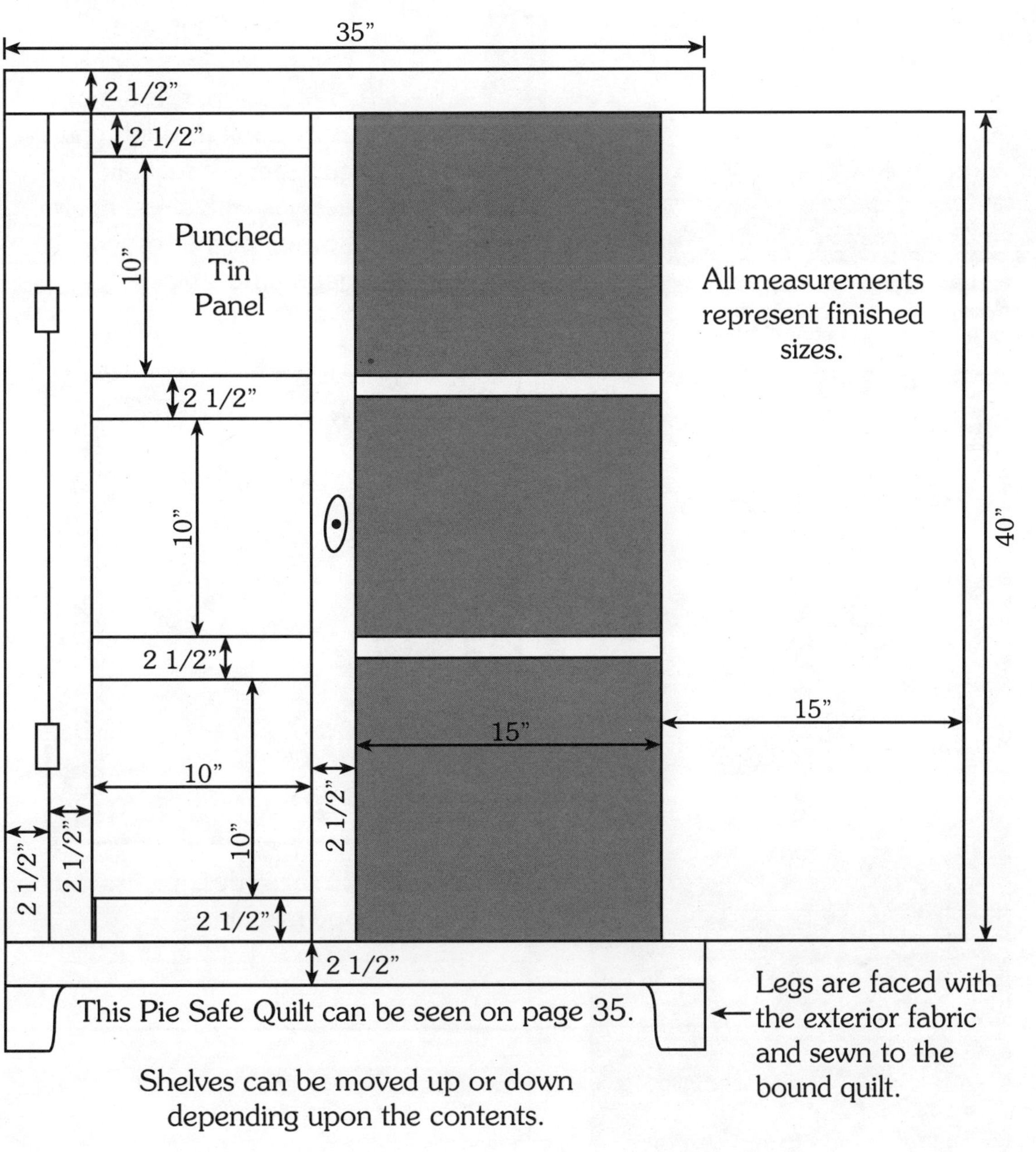

Pierced Tin Panels

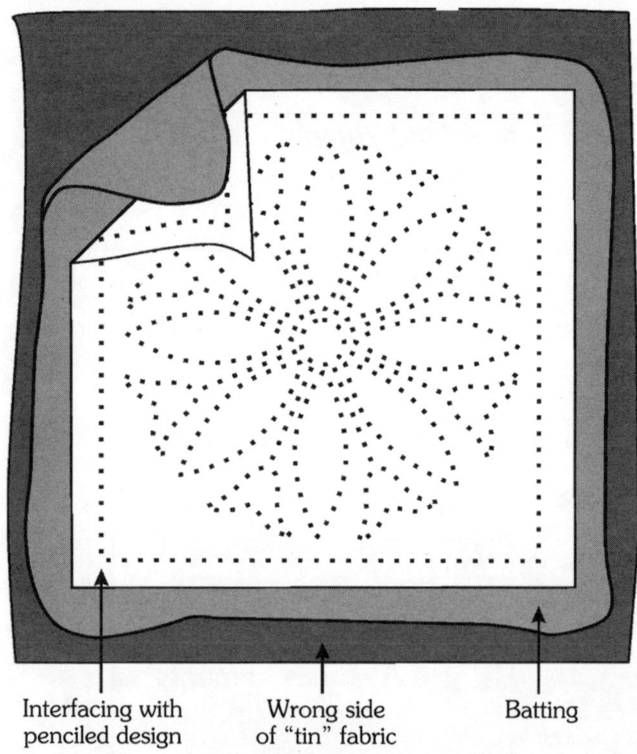

Pie Safes with pierced tin panels were used as food storage cupboards before the ice box was introduced. While air circulated through the doors, insects and dust were kept off the food.

Many of the same designs used in quilting were hammered into panels of tin, copper, brass or zinc. Look through your quilt stencils for folk designs with stars, hearts, flowers or interesting geometric shapes.

Enlarge any of these designs using a copy machine.

The finished measurements of any particular cupboard will be based upon the size you have chosen for the pierced panel.

Thanks to James Palotas, a master craftsman, for sharing his authentic designs. For further information about ordering actual pierced metal panels for your home, contact him at:

Country Accents
P.O. Box 437
Montoursville, PA 17754
Phone: 570-478-4127

Lots More To Be Shelved

Plants and Flowers

1. Flowered fabrics printed on a background that is the same color as the fabric chosen as the shadow behind the shelf, work the best. For example, use pink roses surrounded by black if the background is black. For a more interesting bouquet, make several faced appliques featuring groups of flowers and overlap them above the vase (see pages 34,38 and 44).

2. Silk ribbon flowers are beautiful and just a few will accent a tiny bud vase. There are several books on the market explaining this technique.

3. Fill a vase with flowers made with fabric yo-yos or even buttons.

4. Appliqued flowers, such as those used on Baltimore Album quilts are perfect.

5. By ironing a fusible webbing to the back of a flowered fabric, single blossoms and leaves can be cut out and fused in place. The holly leaves on page 48 were constructed from two fabrics fused together, cut individually and outlined with Fray Check.

6. Purchased silk flowers can be used. On the Wedding Quilt I included a silk wedding bouquet which I attached by stitching velcro circles to both the bouquet and the quilt. The bouquet can be removed when the quilt is folded.

Folded Quilts and Fabric

At last, a purpose for those quilt blocks without partners! Page through old magazines for photos in which stacks of quilts are displayed.

The Search is on!

1. Do you have any quilt blocks from that beginners' class that never quite made it to the bed?

2. Find those old blocks that you could not resist purchasing at that last quilt show or yard sale.

3. How about those quilted vests, bags, and skirts that you no longer wear? Take a deep breath and pick up your scissors!

4. Recycle pillow tops that no longer match your color scheme.

Let's Begin!

1. Cut the background rectangle that the quilts or fabric will rest in front of.

2. Beginning at the bottom of the shelf, layer each quilt block tucking the lower edge under. The upper edge is covered by the block on top of it. Make sure the horizontal folds are not too straight and resemble an actual stack of quilts.

3. Once satisfied either hand or machine stitch these "folded quilts" to the background rectangle and proceed with the construction of the shelf.

4. In stacking folded homespuns or fabrics, fold the cloth in half lengthwise with right sides together and seam across both ends, partially closing the open side.

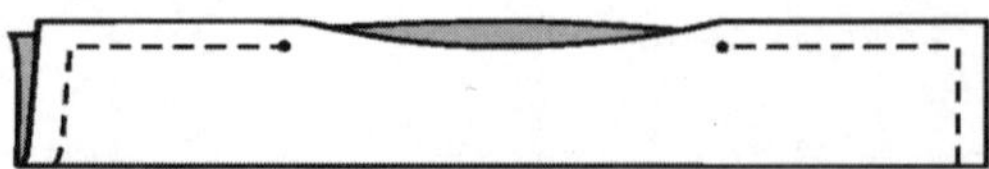

5. Turn these tubes to the right side and begin arranging them on the shelf. Manipulate the folds for a more realistic image.

Above the Shelf

If you choose to place a favorite antique on top of a shelf, it would have to be sewn onto a piece of fabric that represented the wall behind it. I would extend this fabric along the side of the quilt as in the drawing below.

Half of a Quilt or More

Perhaps - just perhaps - you have half of a Lone Star quilt in a box. Wouldn't that look great "hanging" behind your shelf or pie safe. Seam the quilt to the top of the shelf and quilt it as one. Conscience cleared - box emptied! (See Judith's quilt on page 33.)

Personalize with Transfers

Here are some ideas of items that can be scanned or photocopied before being transferred to fabric with an iron or your printer.

1. Photos - postcards - maps - ticket stubs - greeting cards.

2. Awards - diplomas - report cards - birth and wedding certificates - invitations.

3. Food items - cereal and snack boxes - labels from canned food (favorite soups, vegetables, etc.) - candy wrappers, - a box of tea or coffee.

4. Plates - pottery - silverware from magazines and catalogs.

5. “Stuff” from the kitchen, garage, desk - box of matches - packet of seeds.

6. Book covers - opened books.

7. Instructional books and boxes from children’s toys.

Cross Stitch and Doilies

1. Tiny cross stitched pictures can be framed as outlined in the section on photographs.

2. Doilies can be sliced and seamed between shelf boards adding a soft, delicate appearance to the quilt.

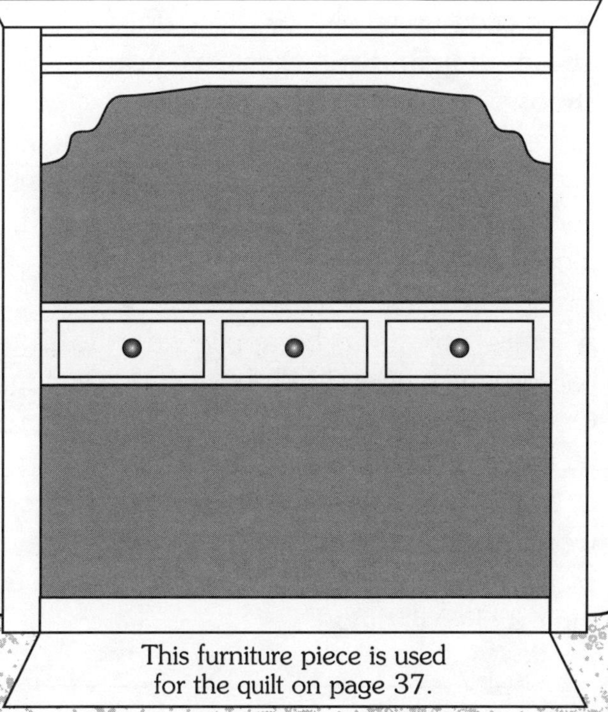

This furniture piece is used for the quilt on page 37.

Shelf Construction

1. Choose a particular shelf arrangement and determine the size or sizes of the shelves in both height and width. Uniform shelves, as on page 21, can be begun once the shelf height is established. The width is often finalized only after one or two shelves are completed.

2. Faced appliques will be sewn directly onto the background fabric used to represent the shadowy interior of the shelf. By cutting this rectangle or several rectangles and pinning them to a design surface you can begin to place your appliques and move them about. In the Family Photo quilt (page 44) each rectangle was sliced and photos, bottles, etc. were moved about until a little voice said, "Enough is enough - sew!" (Fig. A)

Fig. A

Background rectangles upon which appliques will be sewn.
All sizes represent cut sizes - not finished sizes.

3. On a shelf with both pieced (books) and appliqued objects, first construct the pieced units. Move these units about distributing them as you choose.

4. Those areas left blank must be filled with background fabric cut to the height of the pieced units. (Fig. B)

Fig. B

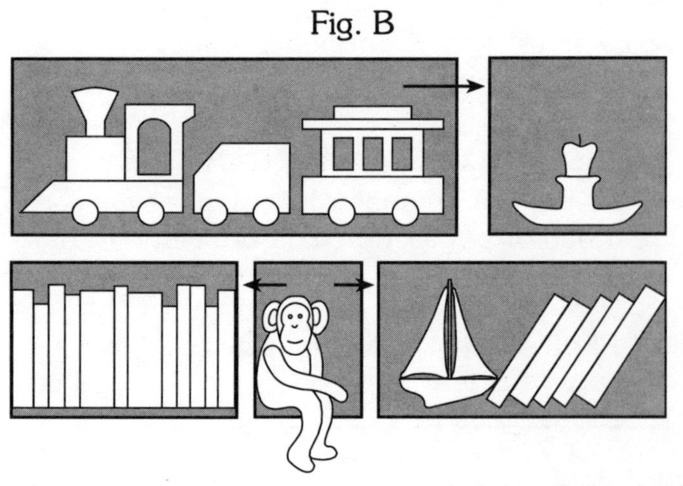

5. Place objects to be appliqued onto these background pieces, 1/4" above the lower edge. Once positions are finalized, stitch them down by machine using a pin stitch (_ _ |_ _| _ _) or a narrow zig-zag. Transparent nylon thread works well. Objects composed of very tiny pieces can be ironed onto the background using fusible webbing.

6. After a width is determined each shelf must be sized. An extra book or slice of background fabric can easily be added (or cut away) until all the shelves are identical.

7. By examining many of the furniture drawings throughout this book you can determine which "fabric boards" will be sewn first and which will overlap. "Building" this quilt will follow the same sequence as that used in making actual furniture.

8. First horizontal boards (fabric strips usually cut 2" in width) will be cut to the determined width. Be alert and cut the fabric so that it best represents a wood-like grain line. **All boards are cut with the grain, not across the grain.**

9. Moldings add depth and define the shelf edge. Slice a strip of board fabric 1 1/4" wide and another (if desired), 1 3/4" wide by the length of the shelf. Press each of these in half horizontally. (Fig. C) A piece of yarn can be slipped into the folds for added dimension.

10. Stitch this folded strip or strips to the shelf board. Actually you will be adding a piping to the seam. (Fig. D)

Note: If possible attach a walking foot to the sewing machine when sewing all the piping and shelf boards. This helps to prevent puckering.

11. Sew this strip with molding to the bottom of each shelf. Below the bottom shelf you may prefer a wider board. (Fig. E)

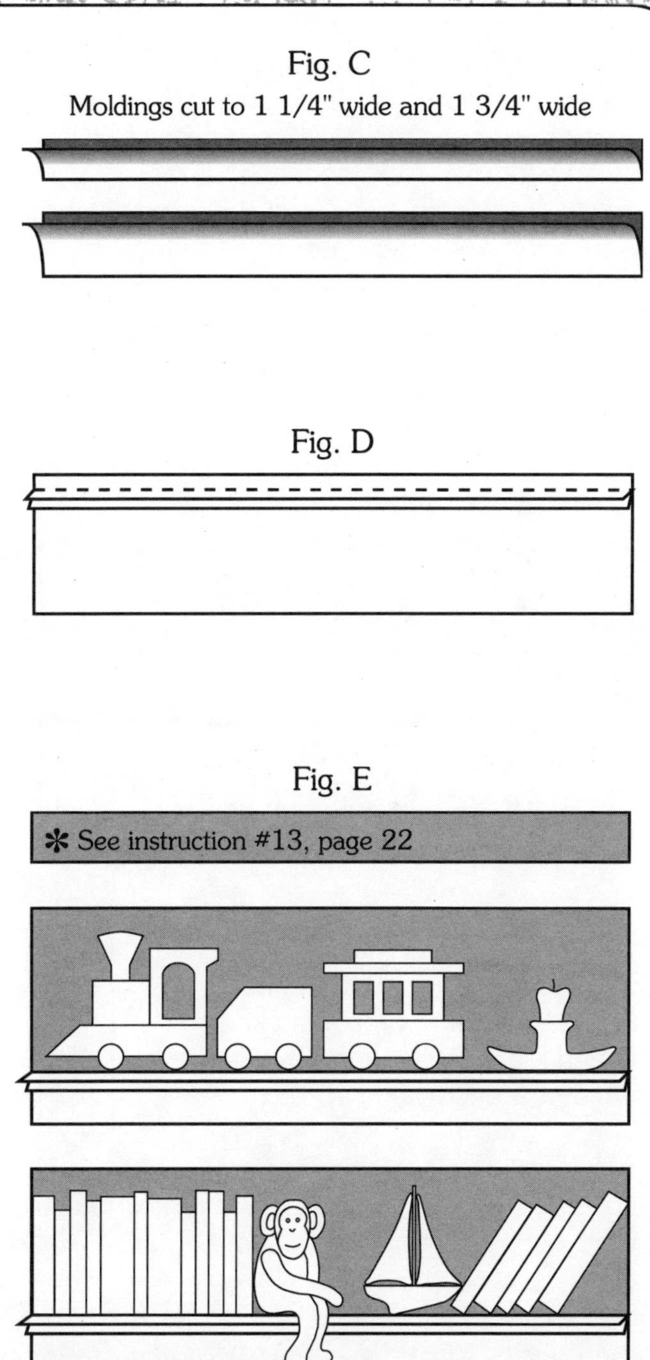

12. A decorative insert (cornice) can be added above the top shelf. Using a narrow folded strip of paper as wide as the shelves, draw the desired shape. Next construct a faced applique by layering two strips of the "wood" fabric with right sides together and stitching along the curves in the drawn shape. Trim, turn, and press. (Fig. F)

Fig. F

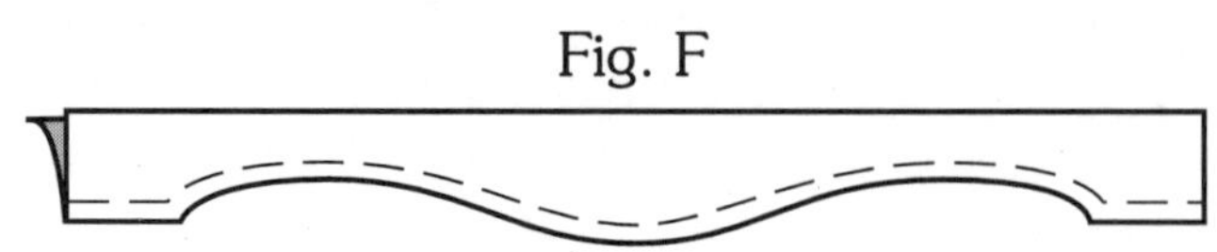

Fig. G

13. Depending upon the height of the objects on your top shelf you may need to add an additional strip of background fabric to accommodate this decorative facing. (* on Fig. E, page 21) Pin this faced shape to the top shelf and top stitch along the lower edge.

14. Sew all the shelves together and then add the side strips which I usually make slightly wider than the horizontal boards. (Fig. G)

15. Now add the very top of this shelf. Varying the width of several strips of the wood-like fabric with molding (folds of piping) tucked between the seams, gives the appearance of a decorative cornice.

16. The sides of this cornice can be squared off or slanted. Examples can be seen in the center quilt gallery.

Fig. H

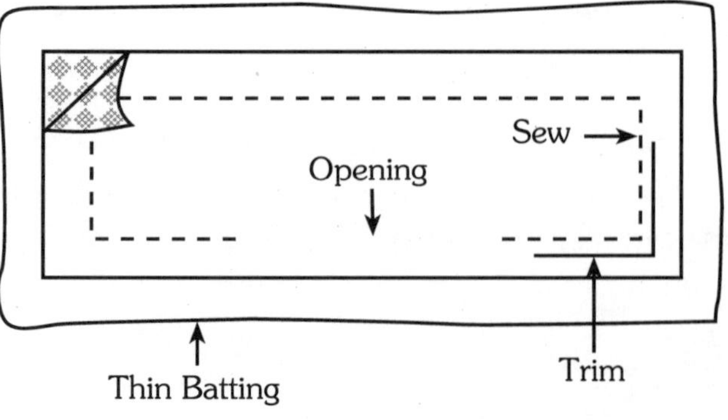

17. Drawers, if desired, are to be added to the quilt at this time. Construct each drawer as you would a patched pocket. Layer two fabric rectangles with right sides together and slip a thin piece of batting underneath. Pin and stitch around the perimeter allowing an opening on one side for turning. Trim, turn, press, and stitch the opening closed. (Fig. H) Applique the drawers to the quilt by hand or machine. Large Victorian buttons make perfect knobs.

18. Now that your masterpiece is complete it must be quilted.

a. Layer the quilt back, batting (medium weight cotton) and top, and baste or pin.

b. Machine or hand quilt. I first machine stitch along the horizontal shelf lines (above and below - in the ditch) and then outline books and appliques. Much of this sewing is done on the background fabric with the same color thread. When sewing between books, I use transparent nylon threads. Shelf backgrounds are usually quilted with vertical lines.

c. Retracing lines (in the ditch) throughout the basic structure will reinforce realistic furniture lines.

d. Add a sleeve for hanging and bind with the same "wood" fabric.

19. Go out for dinner at your favorite restaurant.

20. Time to design another "piece of furniture" for a friend.

Let's Make A Basket

Doesn't everyone put their children's toys in a plastic clothes basket?

FOLD

1. Draw a basket to the desired size.

2. With a dark marker, trace all the basket lines onto the paper side of freezer paper (3" larger than the drawing).

3. Fuse a piece of tule or netting onto the waxed side of the freezer paper by pressing with a warm iron. Test a small section so that the heat doesn't melt the tule. The basket lines should be visible through the tule.

4. With the tule side up, stitch colored braid (or 1/4" bias tape) over all the basket lines. Braid ends should extend beyond the outer edges. Finish by stitching the braid along the outer edges. Both the top and bottom of the basket on page 43 have 3 rows of braid.

5. Tear away the freezer paper. Only the tule with the stitched braid will remain.

6. Face the basket with the fabric to be used for the shelf background. With the *right side of the basket* (tule + braid) facing the *wrong side of the background fabric*, stitch along the sides and the bottom leaving the top of the basket open.

7. Trim, turn, fold the extra background fabric behind the basket, and fill with appliques. Tack the appliques in place. Stitch the basket onto the shelf.

(See quilt on page 43.)

Childhood Favorites

Check the library
for lots more dinosaurs.
(See quilt on page 43.)

This block can be pieced with 3 fabrics (a light, a medium, a dark) Add a motif from a children's print and face the entire block.

(See quilt on page 43.)

I used wooden buttons for wheels. Audition several for the perfect color and size.

(See quilt on page 43.)

Yarn, baling twine, or string can be used for the mane and tail.

(See quilt on page 43.)

Most patterns included in this section are full size; however, they can easily be enlarged or reduced to meet specific requirements. I enlarged this fellow to fill the shelf.

(See quilt on page 43.)

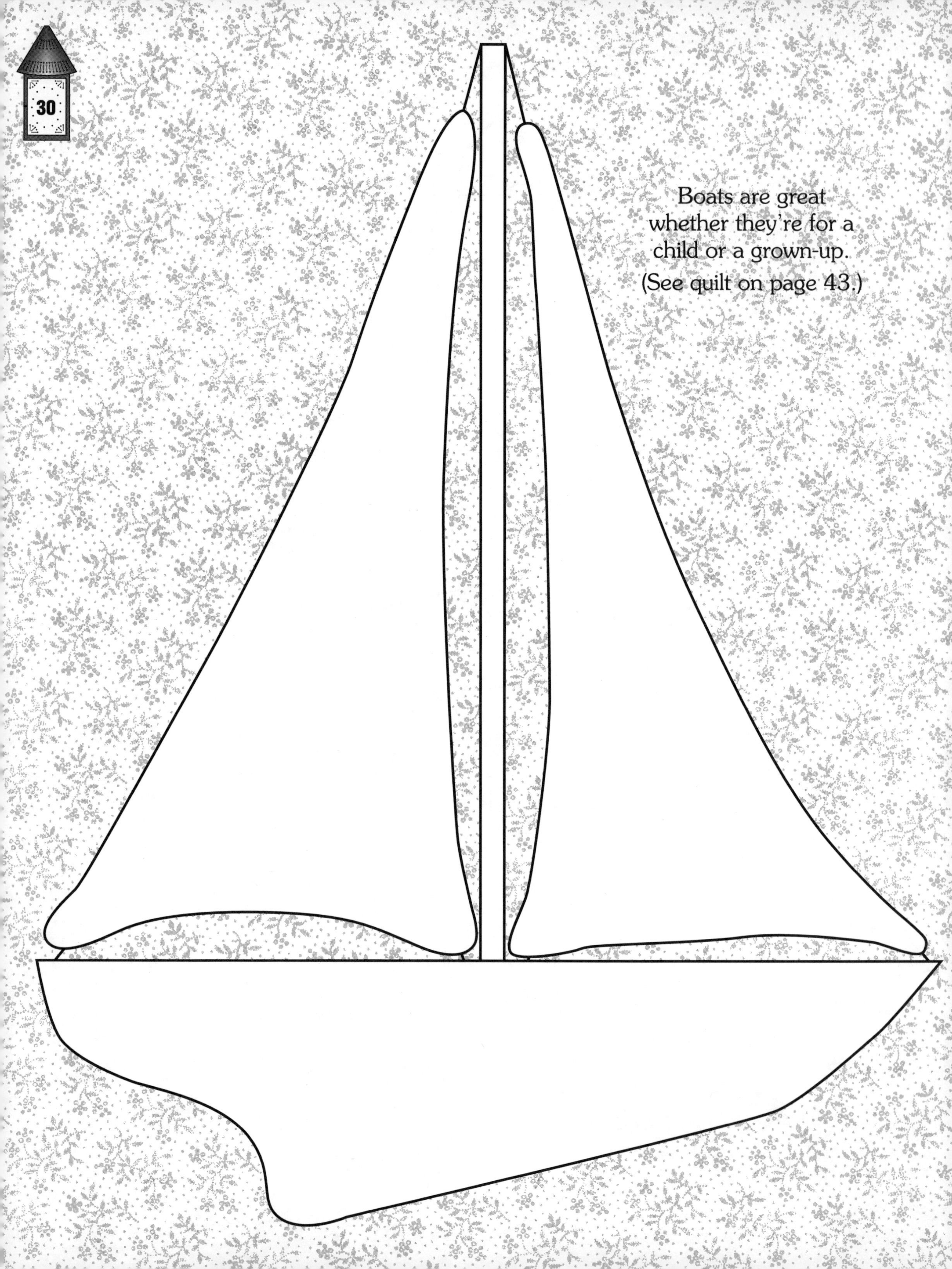
Boats are great
whether they're for a
child or a grown-up.
(See quilt on page 43.)

Models

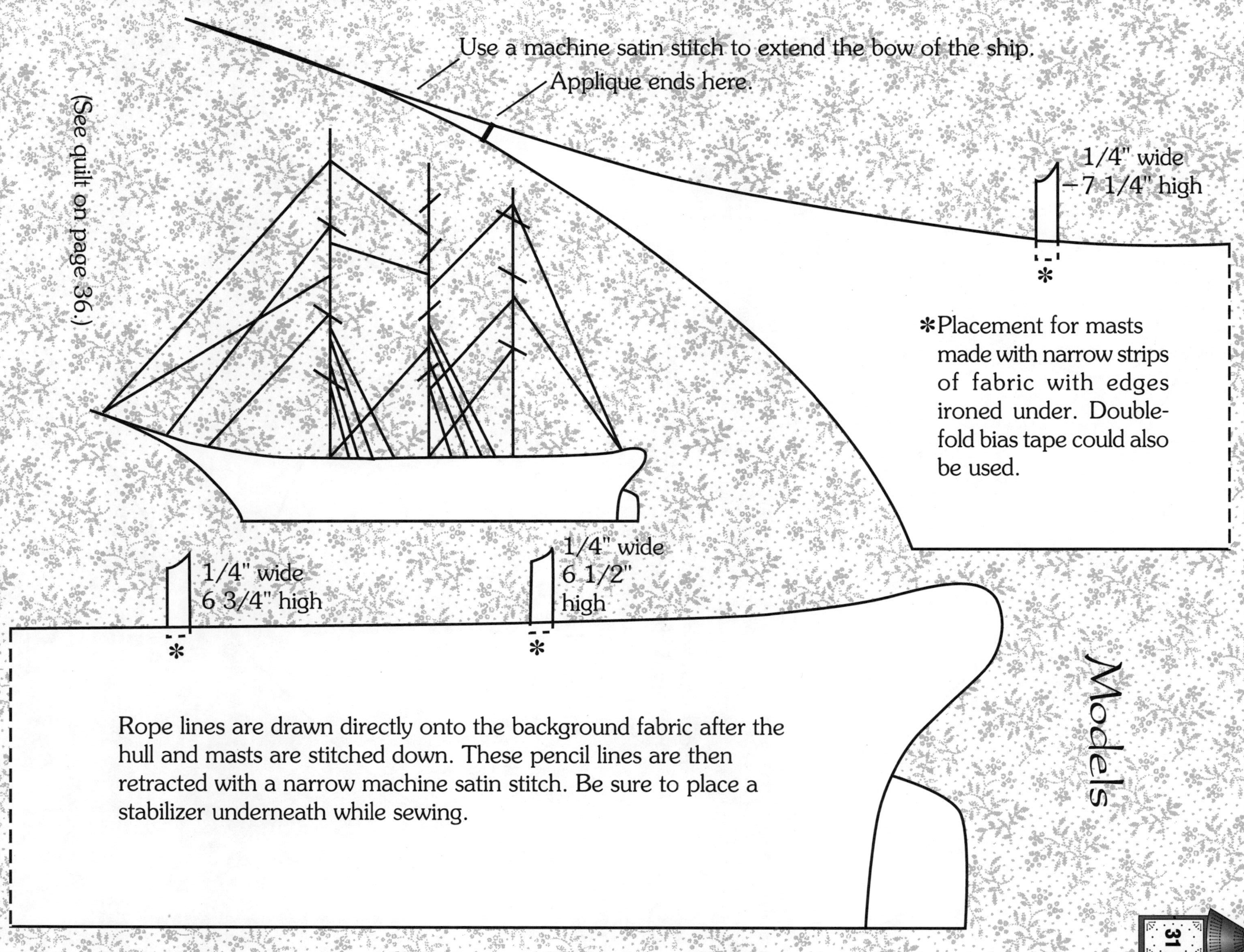

(See quilt on page 36.)

Light up a shelf with a lamp
made from an
irresistible dyed fabric.
I added a pull chain
and an old college pin.
(See quilt on pages 37, 38 and 39.)

"Pennsylvania Pie Safe"
47" x 93"
Judith Youngman
- Antes Fort, PA

In her home, Judith's pie safe houses her collection of reproduction fabrics. The Lone Star quilt was hand quilted and bound before being sewn to the pie safe. On the door hangs a woven tea towel that was fringed.

"Who Can Resist an Antique Sale?" • 37" x 48" – author

Can you find an unfinished crazy patch or a tiny cross-stitch tucked away? Time to put them to use.

"Safe Keeping for my Favorite Quilts" • 47" x 45" – author

This pie safe is filled with leftovers - part of a vest, part of a tote, part of a doll and leftover quilt blocks.

"Teddy Bear" applique by Deborah Konchinsky - The Critter Pattern Works

Basket from quilt on page 39

"Retirement Dreams" • 48" x 38" – author

This light colored frame really brightens up my husband's office.

Here's John's boot from quilt on page 39.

"Shelve Those Ties - Jim" • 31" x 37" - author

Yes, all the books, the lamp and the clock are made from Jim's ties.
Here's how: Open the back seam - remove the lining - reserve the labels to use as book titles - iron carefully - face all "tie books" to avoid bias problems (page 6) - check the wrong side of each tie for more fabric opportunities.

"Generations" • 41" x 53" – Norma Milas – Library, PA

Norma's quilt showcases her family from its Italian roots.
On the back of the quilt she has sewn a hand-written history behind each photo.

"Dear John" • 42" x 53" – Veronica Jones – Williamsport, PA

Everything on this quilt evokes a special memory. Books are made from family ties or scanned and transferred to fabric. Those photos that were not shelved were sewn onto the back of the quilt. John searched for his boot for a week while Veronica sketched and stitched.

"Granny's Summer Kitchen" 33" x 60" – author

Keep your eyes open for great novelty prints. The apples, jars, scale and lower basket were real prizes. Do you have an old apron in a drawer?

"That Old Blue China" • 32" x 35" – author

Plates photographed by Gloria Seaman Allen.

All of the pieces of china on the top two shelves were found in magazines and catalogs. After enlarging they were transferred to fabric and faced. Think about photographing your own china and showcasing it on a shelf.

"After the Wedding" • 48" x 73" – author

It takes real courage to slice a wedding gown in half. The armoire door is faced on 3 sides, quilted and sewn to the door frame. Velcro tabs keep it closed. The mirror is made from a shiny knit.

"Childhood Memories" • 49" x 54" – author

Get lots of photo transfer paper for this one. (I used Photo Effects.) The books and all the drawings were reduced. Since the drawings are not framed, I fused two pieces of white fabric together before ironing on the photo. The upside-down monkey underwent major surgery – "de-stuffing". See page 24 to make a basket.

"Family" • 41" x 53" - author

What a perfect anniversary quilt. One quilter told me how her drawers opened (velcro along the top) to reveal lots more photos.

"Treasures"
39" x 51"
Christine Oxenham
Auckland,
New Zealand

Christine came to class with the most shiny assortment of fabric and trims. Look for the organza tissues, gold tassels, a brush with rat-tail braid and lots more.

"In the Beginning – Collectibles #1" • 50" x 58" – author

If you've collected hand-dyed cottons, you've got to make lots of bottles.

"Raton Remembered" • 51" x 64"
Brenda Myers
Picture Rocks,
PA

Brenda insisted on making a fabric ladder even though we all suggested using the one in the garage. Her cupboard is reminiscent of those she has admired in the Southwest.

"Santa's Jelly Cupboard" • 40" x 53" – author

This is the only quilt I've made that has a lighter shelf background.
I did piece in narrow dark strips to add depth. The door was faced and quilted separately,
then added to the cupboard after the binding was sewn.

It's Christmas

(See quilt on page 48.)

Santas' suits can be made from cottons, velvets, wools, or even silks. A variety of beards made from wool, fringed muslin, batting, fake fur or even doll's hair, add to the collection.

Santas

Here's a great idea for showing off all those fancy stitches. Add a mustache and beard made from loops of narrow ribbon for a Crazy Patch Victorian Santa.

(See quilt on page 48.)

After your faced tree is turned and pressed, you might decorate it with buttons and trim.
(See quilt on page 48.)
Here's a simple Santa with a twine belt.
(See quilt on page 48.)

This Santa was made from scraps of wool that were also faced. (See quilt on page 48.)

Antiques

This tin rooster, the base of an antique lightning rod, can be seen on page 33. Since his tail extends beyond the quilt border, two pieces of fabric were fused and a thin piece of wire was sewn to the back of each feather with a zigzag stitch.

Pierced Tin Lantern

Add a loop of rattail (round cord). Before facing, the pierced lines were transferred to the cone and door by taping the design to a window and placing the lantern fabric on top. With a ruler and a fine point permanent marker, the design lines were traced. After each section was faced. I also hand stitched over the design with black thread.

(See quilt on page 40.)

Door Handle

Cupboard Hinges

(See quilt on page 35 and 42.)

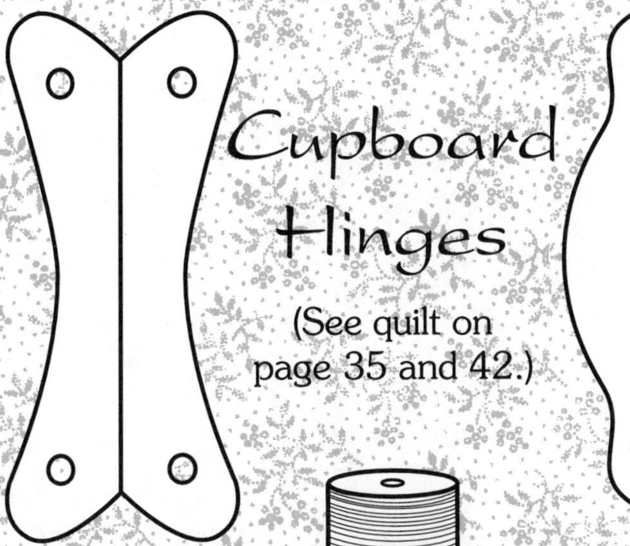

SINGER

Antique Sewing Machine

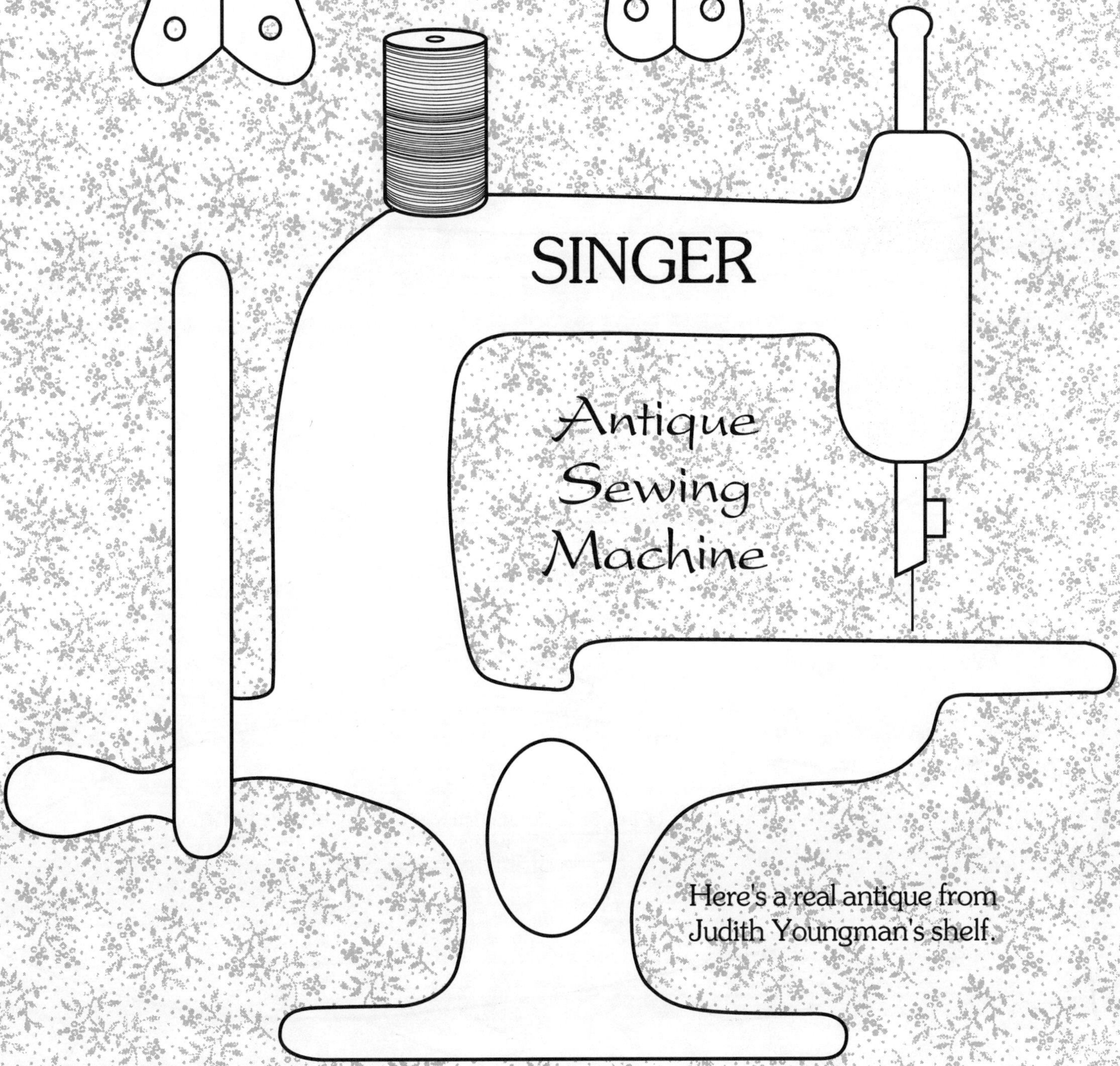

Here's a real antique from Judith Youngman's shelf.

I remember this glass chicken filled with jelly beans each Easter.
(See quilt on page 34.)
Put him on a stand or hang him from a string.
(See quilt on page 36.)

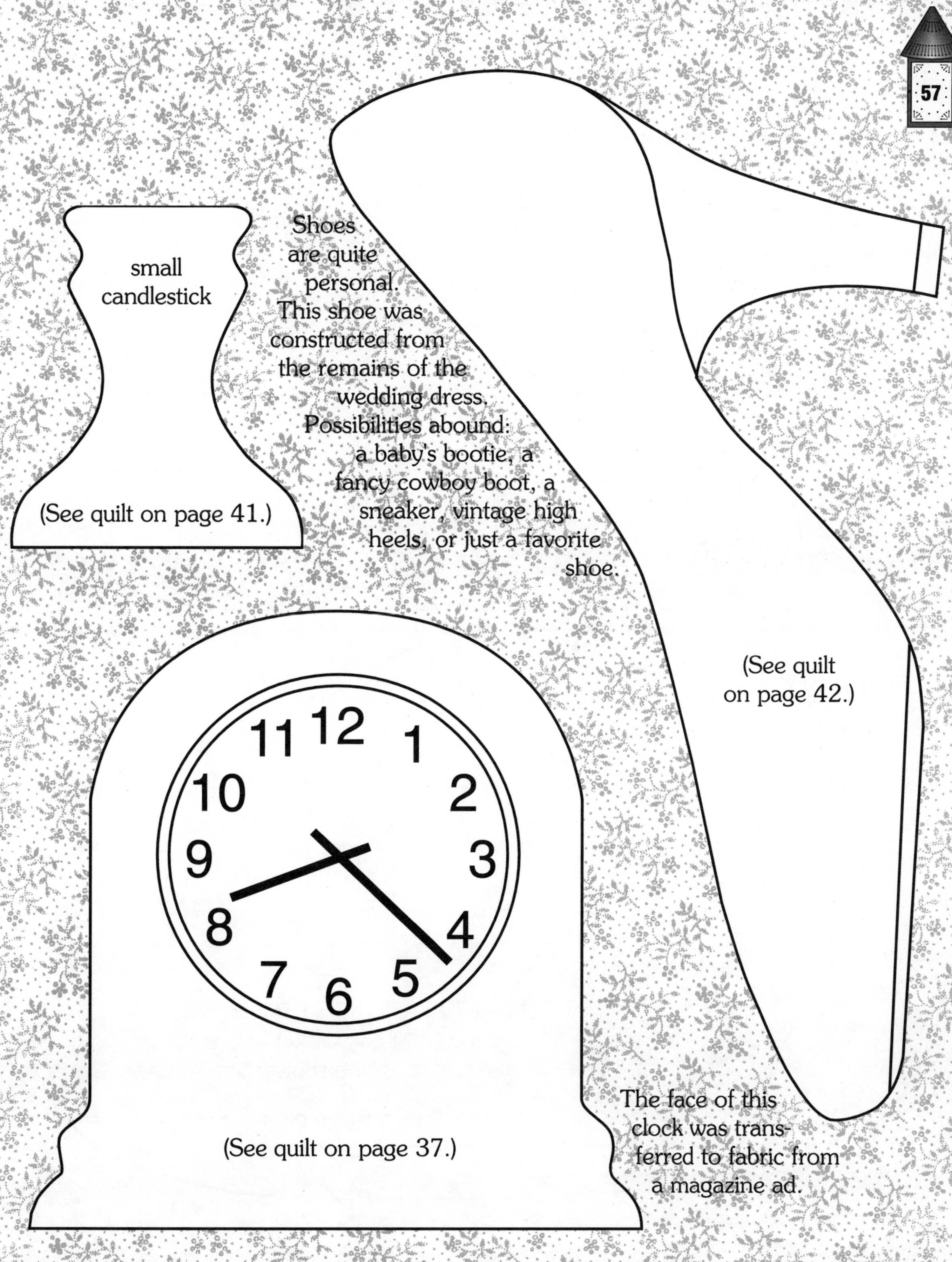
small
candlestick
(See quilt on page 41.)
Shoes
are quite
personal.
This shoe was
constructed from
the remains of the
wedding dress.
Possibilities abound:
a baby's bootie, a
fancy cowboy boot, a
sneaker, vintage high
heels, or just a favorite
shoe.
(See quilt
on page 42.)
11 12 1
10 2
9 3
8 4
7 6 5
(See quilt on page 37.)
The face of this
clock was trans-
ferred to fabric from
a magazine ad.

For Him

Fishing Creel - Collect at least a quarter of a yard of any basket weave fabric you spot.

(See quilt on page 36.)

What about Hats?!

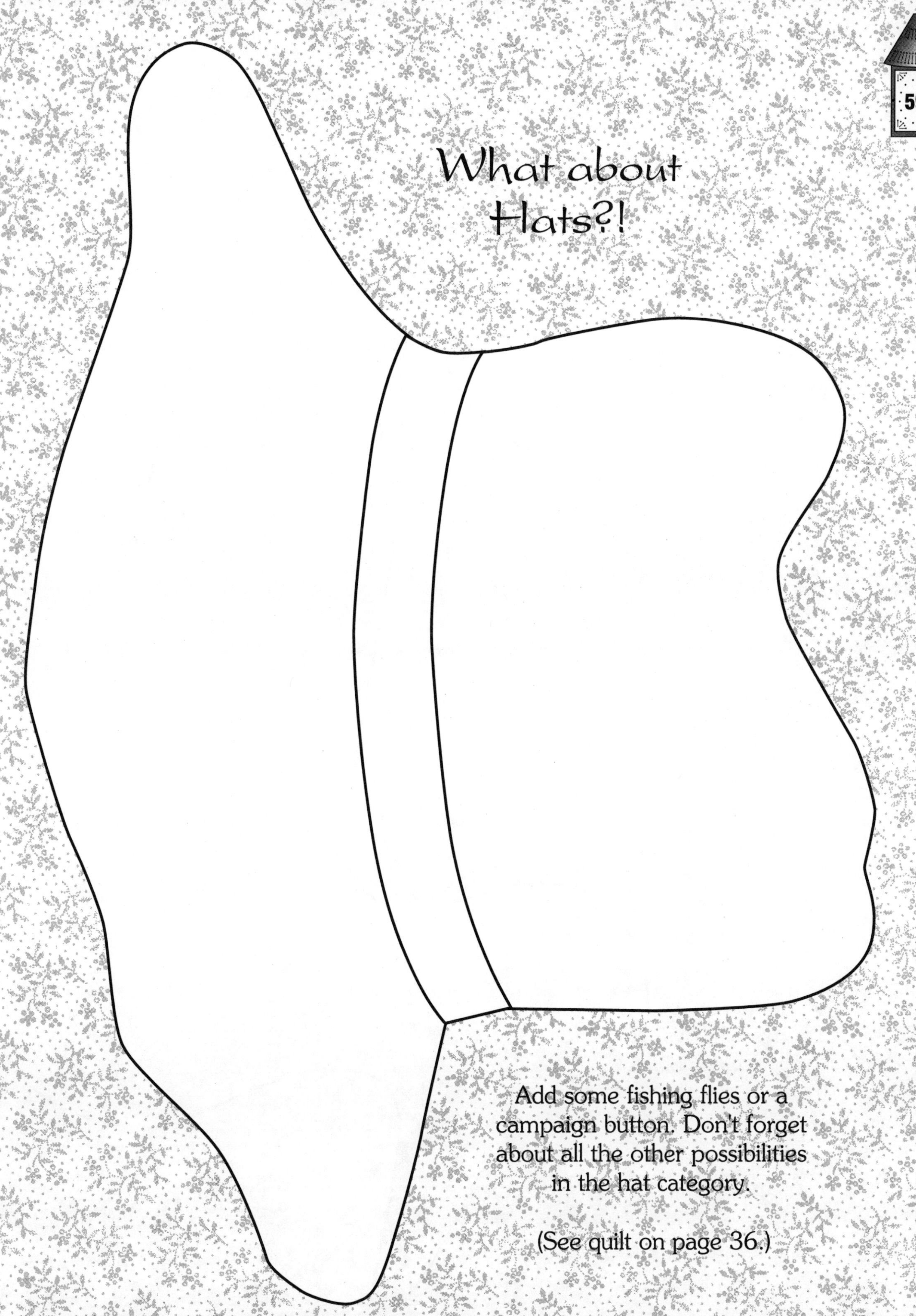

Add some fishing flies or a campaign button. Don't forget about all the other possibilities in the hat category.

(See quilt on page 36.)

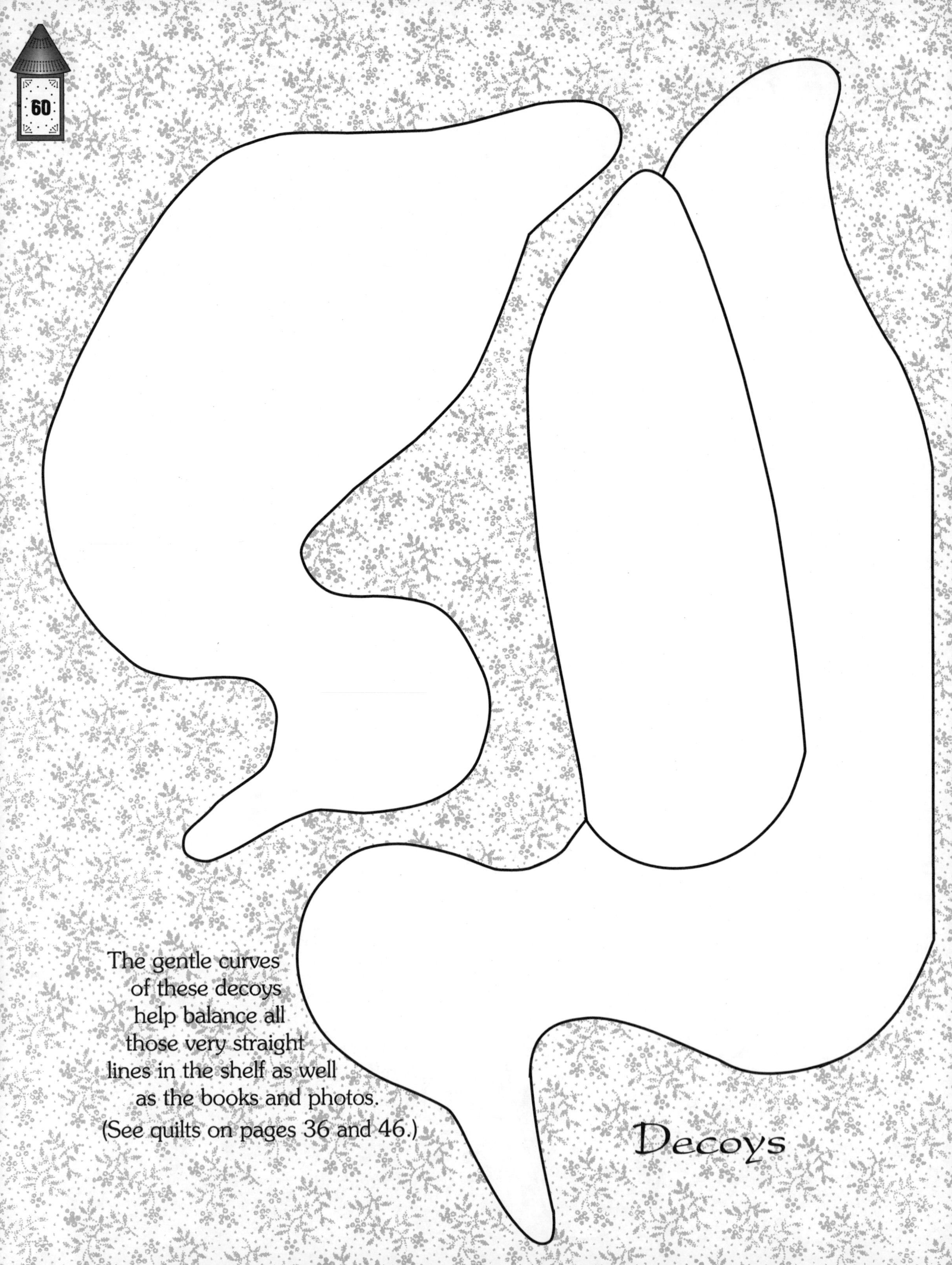

The gentle curves of these decoys help balance all those very straight lines in the shelf as well as the books and photos. (See quilts on pages 36 and 46.)

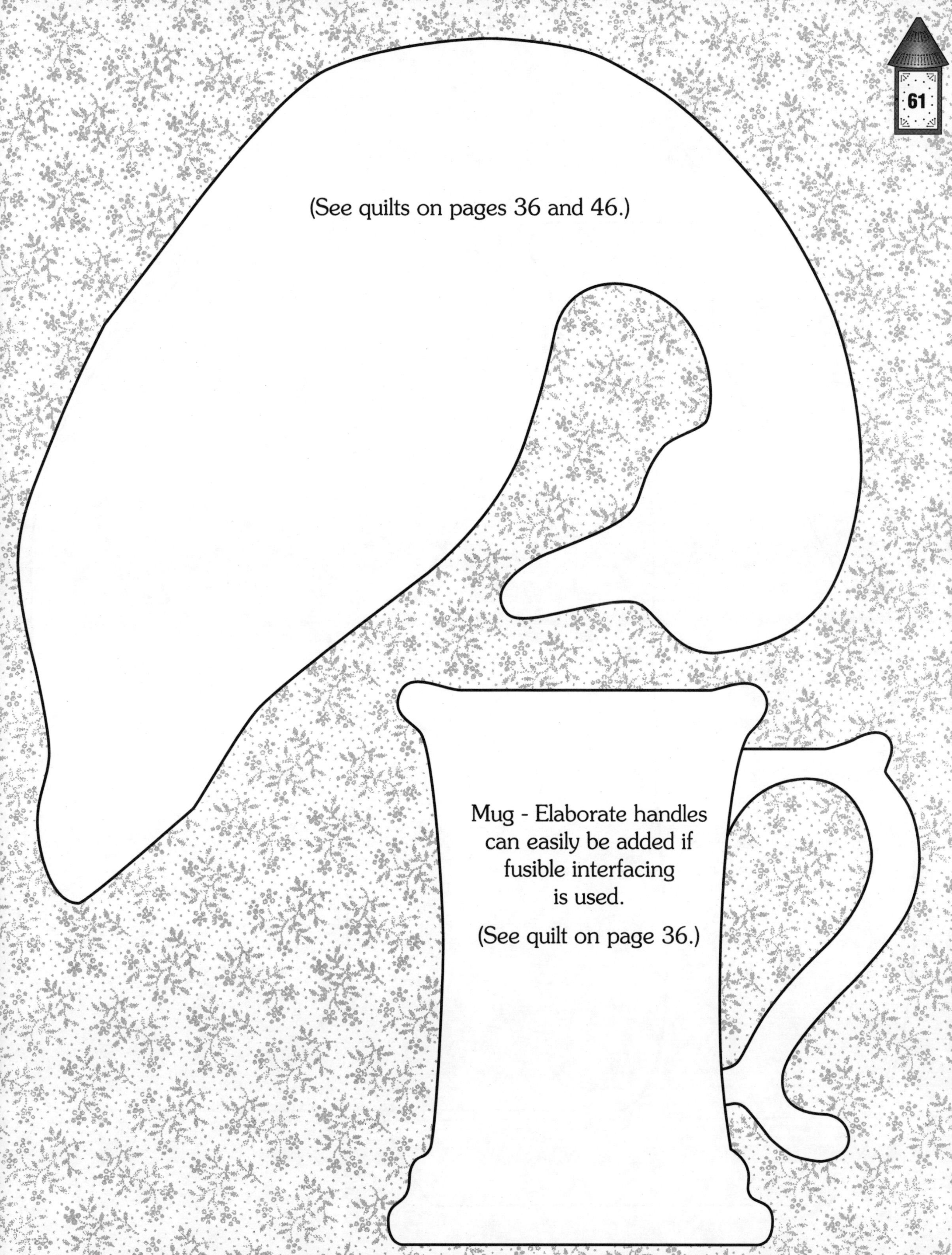
(See quilts on pages 36 and 46.)
Mug - Elaborate handles can easily be added if fusible interfacing is used.
(See quilt on page 36.)

Stoneware Crocks

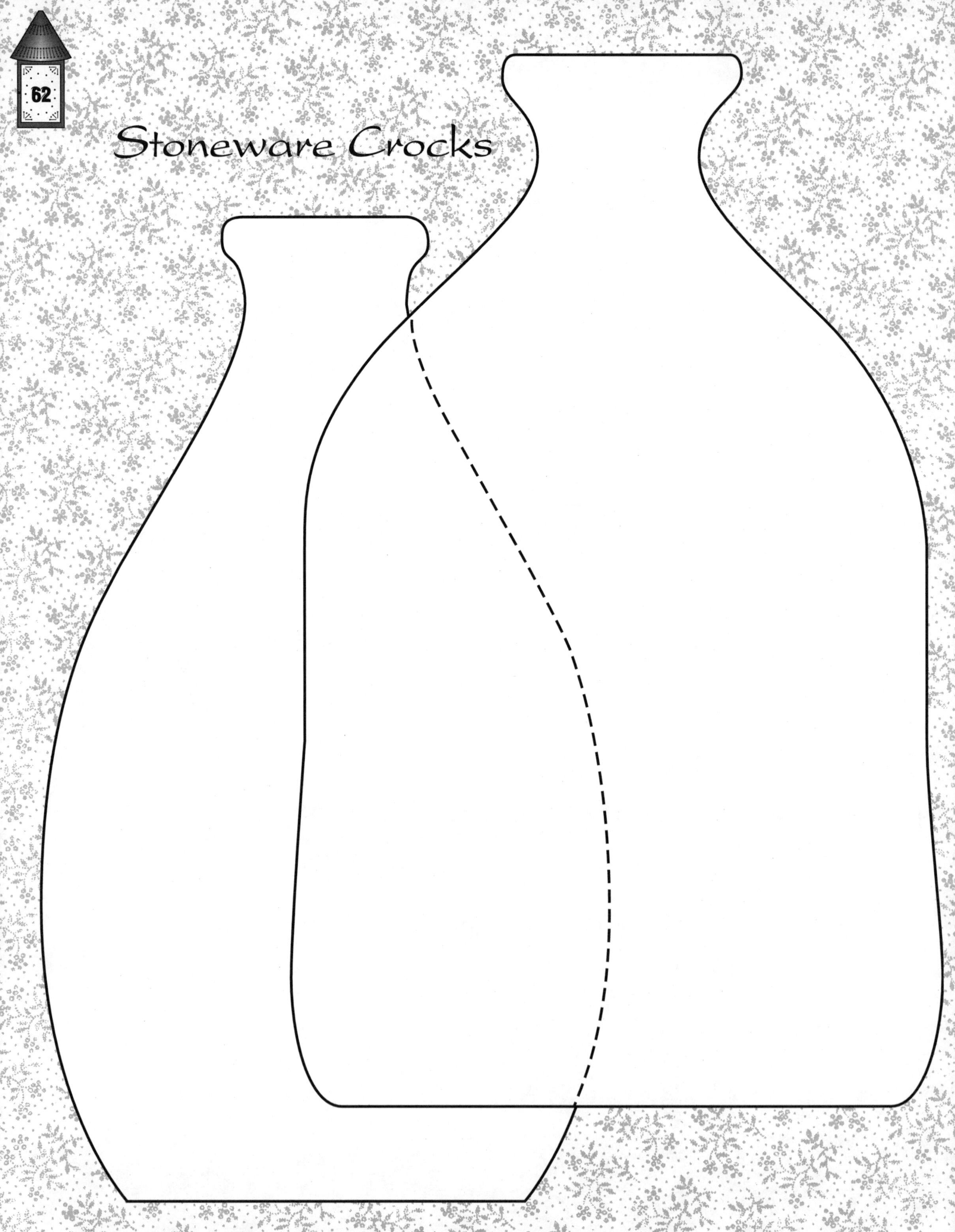

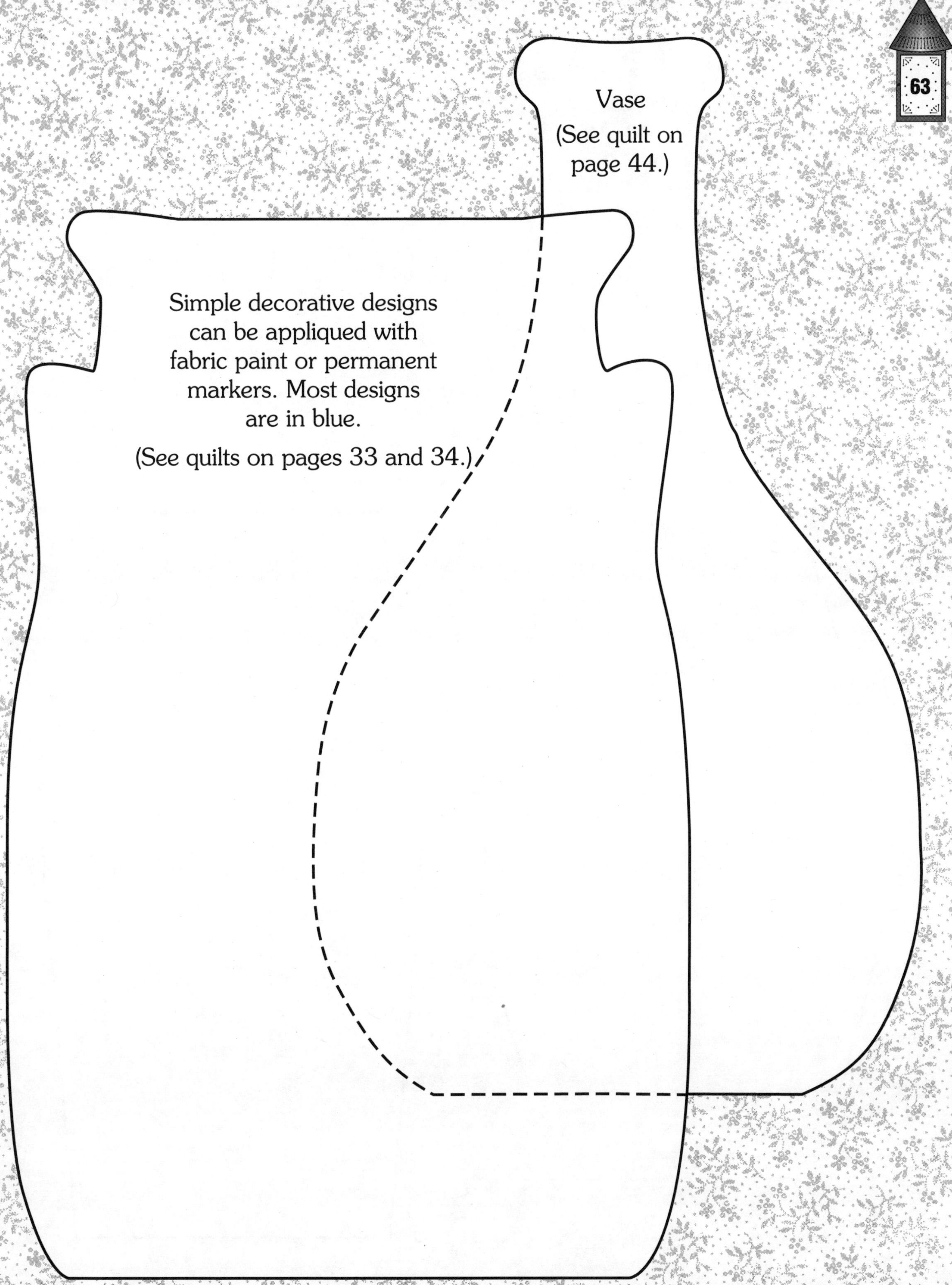
Vase
(See quilt on
page 44.)
Simple decorative designs
can be appliqued with
fabric paint or permanent
markers. Most designs
are in blue.
(See quilts on pages 33 and 34.)

Examples can be seen on pages 38, 40, 44, 45 and 46.

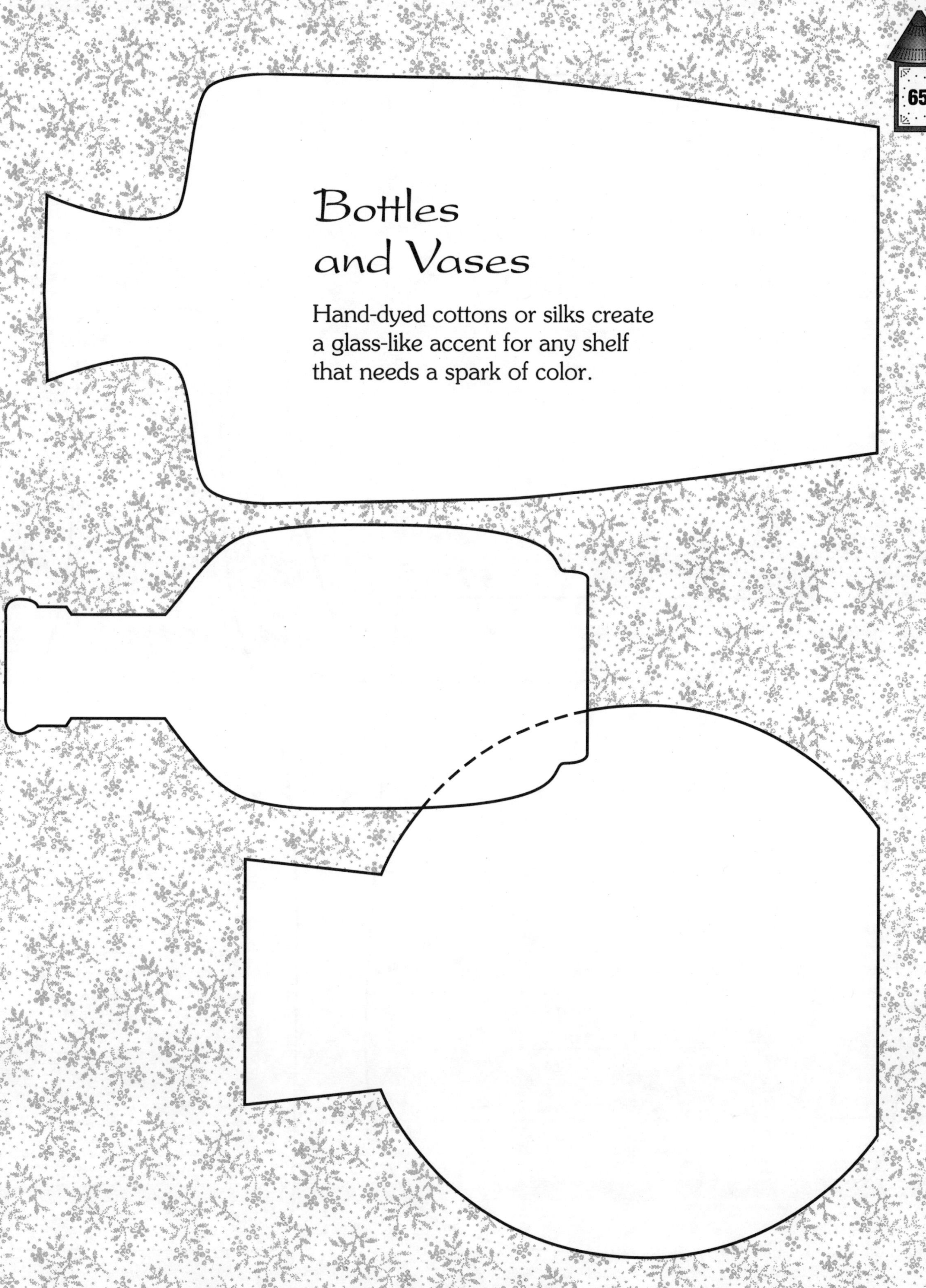

Bottles and Vases

Hand-dyed cottons or silks create a glass-like accent for any shelf that needs a spark of color.

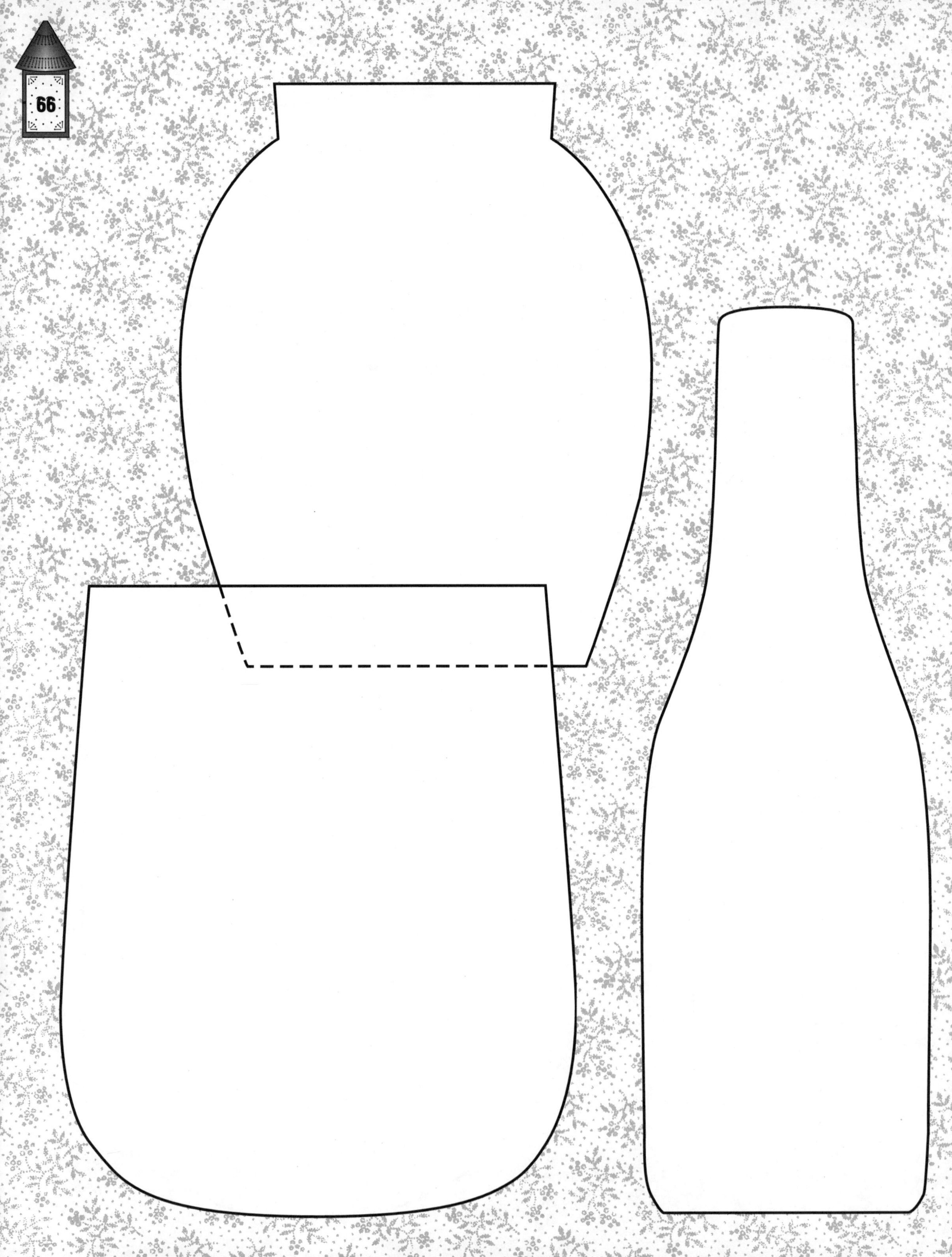

When bottles are grouped and overlap each other, the shelf appears to have depth.

Tall Candlestick -
Great for filling in a tall,
narrow space.
(See quilt on page 42.)

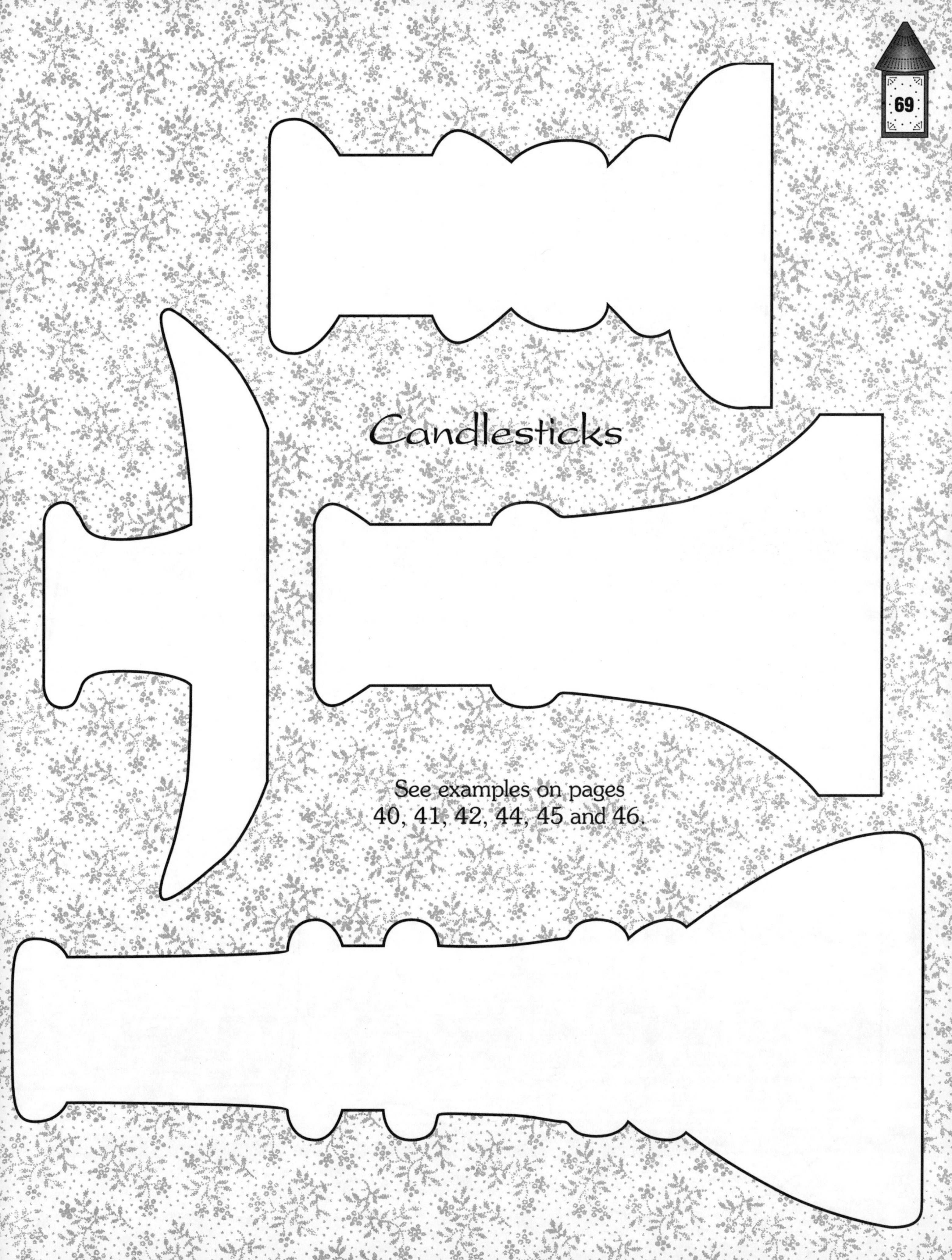

Candlesticks

See examples on pages
40, 41, 42, 44, 45 and 46.

Bowls

Bowls can be made to resemble wood, glass, clay or woven reed.

(See quilts on pages 38, 40 and 46.)

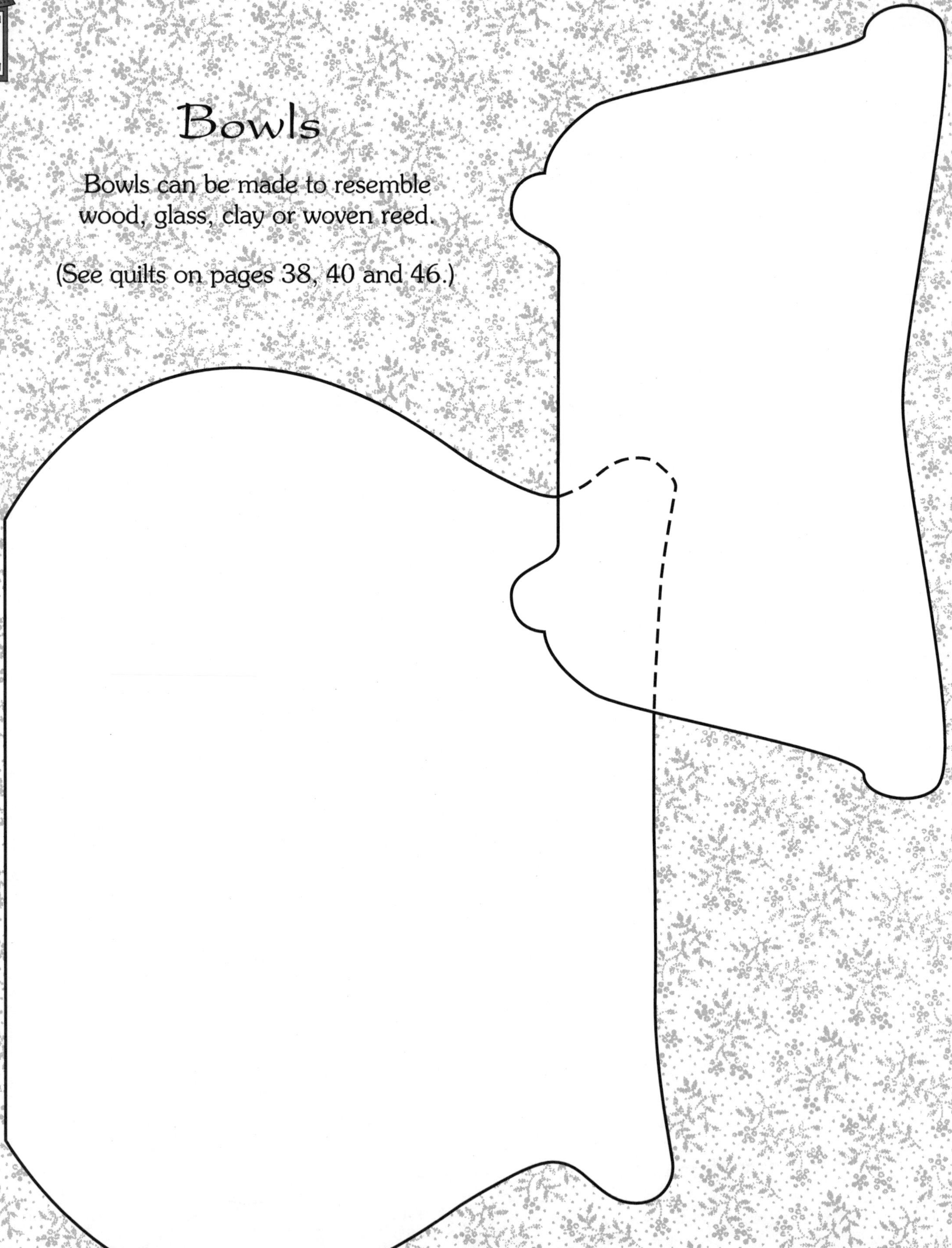

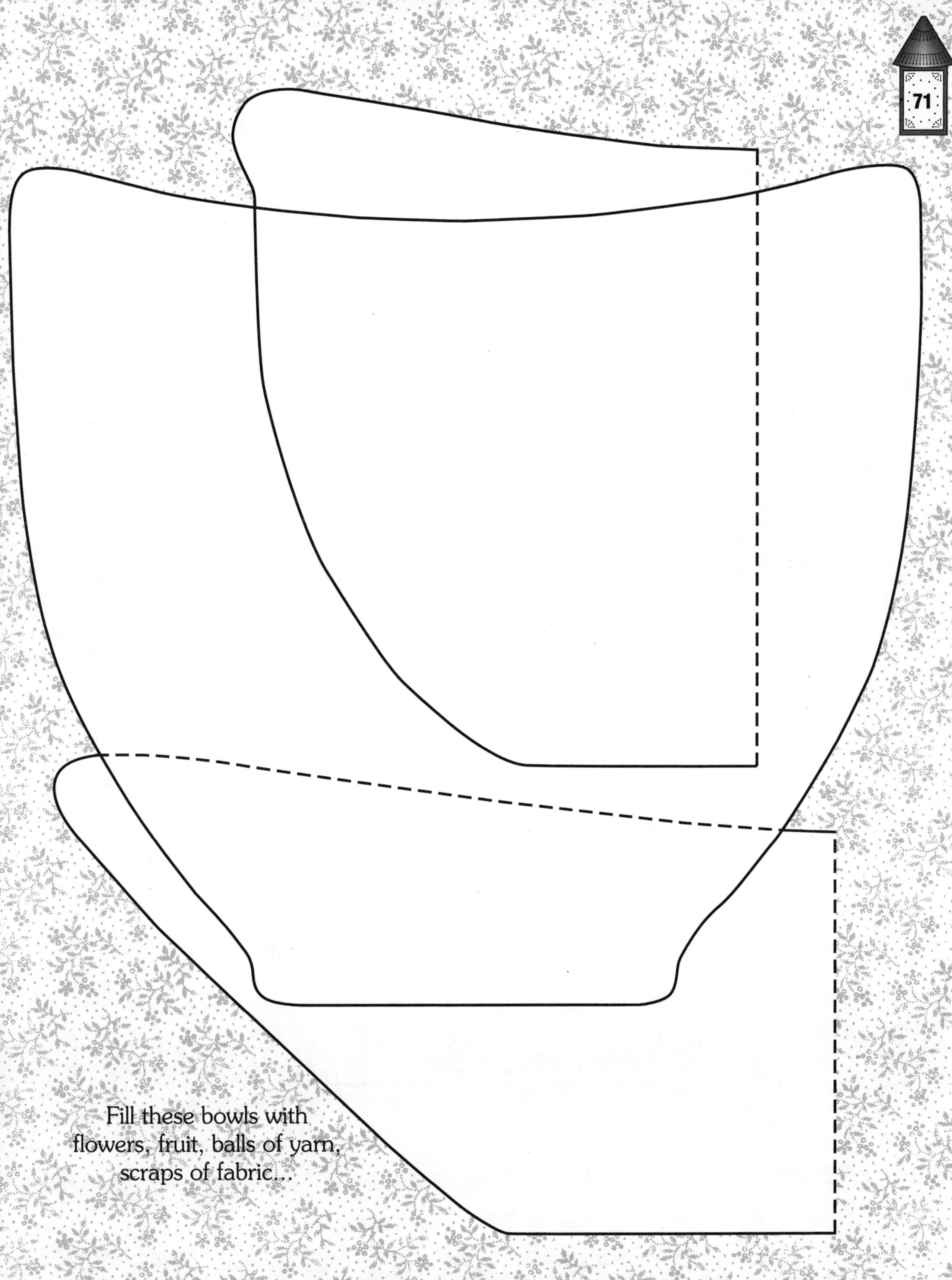
Fill these bowls with
flowers, fruit, balls of yarn,
scraps of fabric...

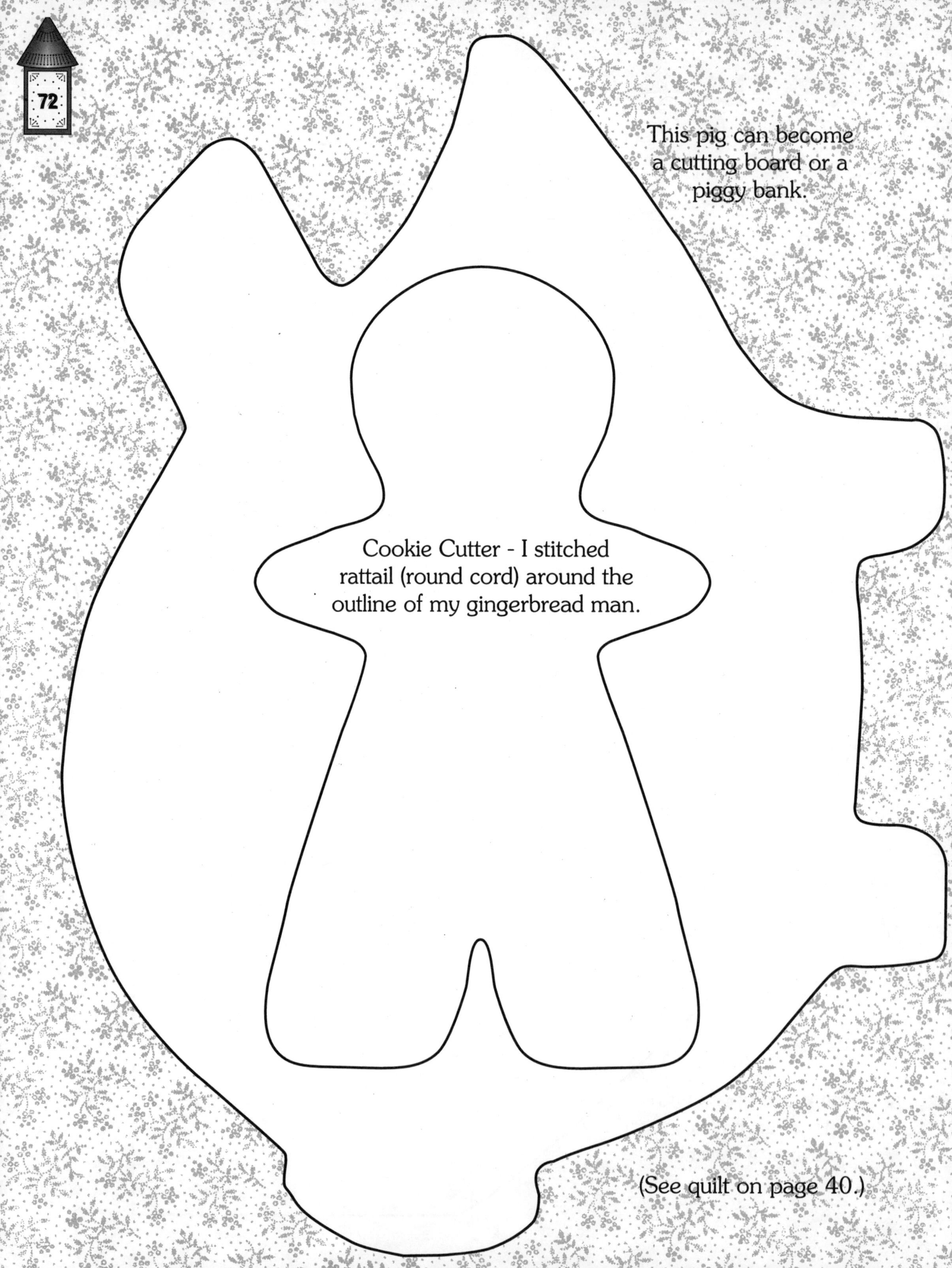

(See quilt on page 40.)

For the Kitchen
Arrange these utensils in a pitcher or a bowl.
Spatula - I simply darkened these circles with a dark permanent marker.
(See quilt on page 40.)

Tea Cup - I machine embroidered a long rectangle of white fabric and then placed the interfacing with each cup outline over the design. The design on each cup was then identical. The handles were fused. Suspend an actual tea cup from your finger to find the proper slant for hanging.
(See quilt on page 41.)
salt shaker
(See quilt on page 41.)
pitcher
(See quilts on pages 40 & 44.)

sugar bowl

fruit bowl

creamer

Teapot - Here's a
great spot for a fabric
with larger motifs -
birds, flowers, people,
scenes, etc.
(See quilt on page 34.)

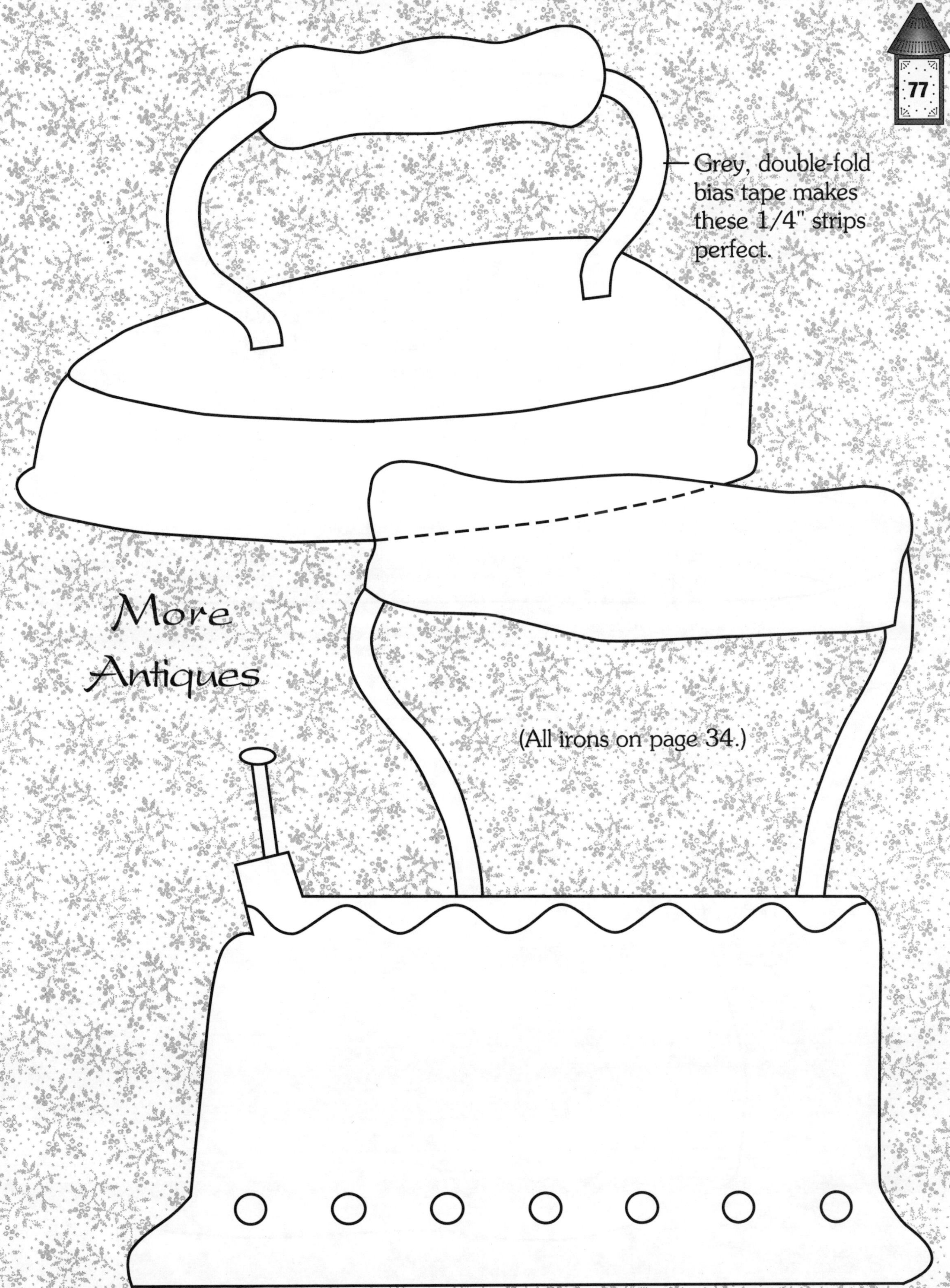
Grey, double-fold bias tape makes these 1/4" strips perfect.
More Antiques
(All irons on page 34.)

Baskets

When there's a space to fill, add a basket. Then fill it with sewing notions, fruit, plants, photos, postcards, letters...

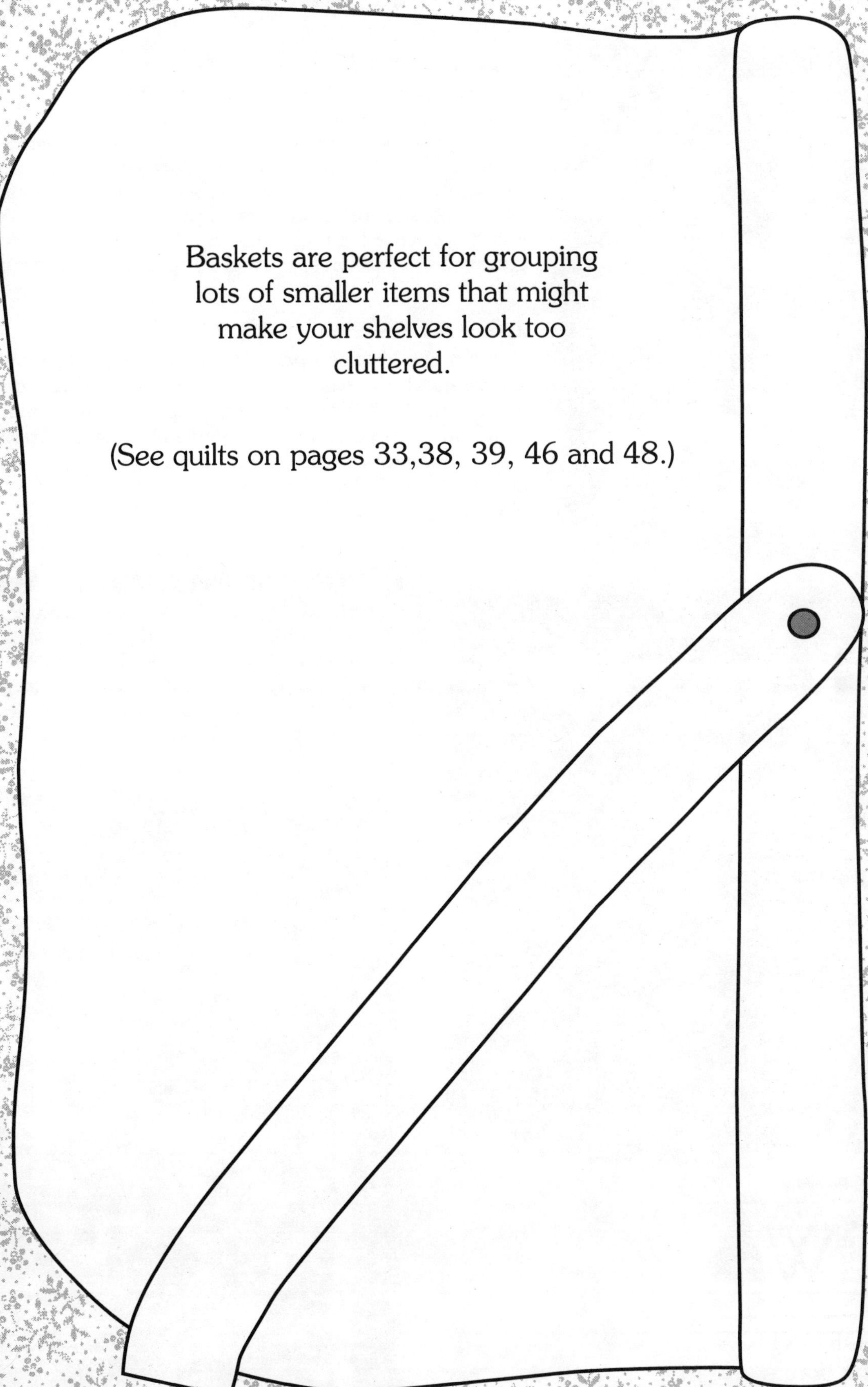

Baskets are perfect for grouping lots of smaller items that might make your shelves look too cluttered.

(See quilts on pages 33,38, 39, 46 and 48.)

Stitch *A Lasting Memory*

KITE REVUE $16.95

Join the new *Kite Revue* with piles of scraps and just one template. As the curtain rises, a chorus of kites will transform into a spectacular display of quilts with dazzling stars, diamonds, pendants, medallions and lots more. Choose one of the designs in the "Program" or choreograph your own quilt on the grid sheets provided. Precise instructions and a colorful quilt gallery full of inspiration will spotlight your performance.

LOG BY LOG $19.95

Capture the look of a primitive folk quilt while visiting with ancestors of the past through the eyes of Lydia Jane. After the binding is stitched you just might have to build a miniature log cabin with pebbles and sticks. Step by step instructions for stitching folk quilts and building model log cabins. Lots of ideas for adding thread drawn trees and applique people and animals.

QUILTING WITH LAURA $12.95

This unique 32-page book features patterns inspired by the "Little House on the Prairie" series. *Quilting with Laura* is designed to help both children and adults create quilts associated with the popular Laura Ingalls Wilder series. Included are 14 block patterns with examples of Album and Friendship Quilts.

Quilting with Laura

Patterns Inspired by the "Little House on the Prairie" series

by Linda Halpin

more books from

For INFORMATION on all our books and to ORDER ON LINE go to **www.rcwpublishing.com**

RR3 Box 43, Old Post Lane, Columbia Cross Roads, PA 16914

800•333•4RCW(4729) FAX 570•549•3332 Email: rcw@epix.net Tel. International: 570•549•3331